CW01265939

A FOOTBALL

REAL ALE

TRAIL

Gareth,
Play up Sky Blues!

(signature) DEC 2020

**'Away' days with Coventry City London
Supporters Club**

the wilderness years 2012-2020

Contents

The Author

Ian Davidson was born in Coventry in 1953. He attended Woodlands school in Coventry where he played First XI football and cricket. His Father took him to his first Coventry City match towards the end of the 1961-1962 season. Jimmy Hill (JH) had arrived by then and the next five years saw his team go from the depths of the 4th Division to the 1st Division (the equivalent of the Premier League today). Ian was hooked. In those early years he attended matches wearing his sky blue scarf, bobble hat and carrying his wooden rattle, singing the Sky Blue Song. The Sky Blues were to stay in the top Division for over 30 years, and despite living in Kent since 1987 Ian has continued to be a season ticket holder and is a regular at away games. Family holidays and international business trips were arranged around the fixture lists.

He was a commercial apprentice at Standard Triumph (British Leyland/Rover) and worked at the Canley, Solihull and Longbridge sites. He moved to work in the other City (of London) for an American bank in 1987, spending a further 25 years in Human Resources in various Financial Services firms before retiring. He is a Fellow of the Chartered Institute of Personnel Development.

One of his claims to fame is that he attended 75% of Coventry City's European games, attending both home games and the 1-6 defeat in Munich. As a then 16 year old his Mum didn't know where Trakia or Plovdiv was and wouldn't let him go. She did promise he could go to the next round if the Sky Blues were to progress. She kept her promise.

Acknowledgements

The recording of these memories would not have been possible without the Coventry City London Supporters' Club (CCLSC) members who gave support and encouragement. These have over the years become friends' and who contributed to these tales of what it really is like to be a football fan, watching your team in the flesh.

Special thanks go to Jim Brown, an honorary member and founder member of CCLSC and the Club's statistician who kindly allowed me to reference his season reviews, to add the football context later in the book.

Thank you to Barry Chattaway, Adrian Hawthorne, Robin Ogleby and Rob Stevens for the photos of CCLSC members from all around the country.

I would like to pay special appreciation to John Bryant (JB) and Phil Wynn Owen who tore through the first drafts in record time, for their careful reading and advice over the text.

Thanks to my wife, Chris, who became a football widow every Saturday, daughter Nikki and son Mark for their patience and words of encouragement. A special thanks to Nikki and son in law Sean for their help and advice on the design and layout.

I would like to thank the Campaign For Real Ale (CAMRA) for the use of their pub photo's and descriptions, and local branch officials for their help with finding suitable pubs in their areas that met our pub criteria. Of course a big thank you to the landlords for their warm welcome when we visit their pubs.

Thanks also go to the Football Ground Guide for the use of the photos and descriptions of the grounds visited. Additional information has been obtained from the various Club websites.

Whilst every effort has been made to trace owners (for copyright permission) for all the material used, I wish to apologise for any parties that have not received due acknowledgement.

Foreword

Coventry City London Supporters Club (CCLSC)

On Monday evening, 22 November 1976, eleven young Coventry supporters gathered at the King's Arms in Poland Street, Soho, in central London. They asked each other if they had been to Villa Park on Saturday, managed to get hold of a copy of the "Pink" or even watched the TV highlights on Sunday afternoon with Huw Johns?

Most likely they only got the condensed version in London on the Big Match and whatever was reported in the national papers.

Something needed to be done to meet the needs of long-distance supporters. Colin Heys' initiative became a reality that night and the Coventry City London Supporters Club (CCLSC) was born.

CCLSC celebrate their 45th Anniversary in 2021.

Even for those living away from Coventry, they are still Sky Blues fans. If they can get to a game or two, it could mean going on their own, sitting in a pub for lunch beforehand and then watching the game. It can take the shine off the day. For over 40 years CCLSC has arranged group train travel and a match ticket collection service for its members. Regular travellers meet before games at a designated pub for a pint or two.

CCLSC are members of the Association of Provincial Football Supporters Clubs in London (APFSCIL) and the Football Supporters Federation (FSF).

Membership is currently (November 2020) just over the 430 mark with members from London, the South East and beyond. It is the oldest Coventry City Supporters Club. It has three classifications of membership.

Firstly, Members who pay an annual membership fee and are provided with group travel, away match ticket ordering and collection, and invitations to member only social events, often with Club officials.

Secondly, UK based Associates who receive the newsletter and other communications without purchasing membership. It is recognised that not all long distance supporters are able to travel regularly to games, but want to stay in touch.

The third category is our international based members. In 1995 **Sky Blues International (SBI)** was founded following an initiative by the then CCLSC Chair, Jonathan Strange and Joe Elliot from the Football Club. Membership is complementary to anyone living permanently outside the UK. We have members situated all over the globe. Many originated from the Coventry area, supporting the Sky Blues before emigrating living and working in countries like Australia, Canada, most European countries, New Zealand and the USA. We have individual members in thirty or so countries like the UAE, Uganda and Thailand. The largest group of members with no apparent link to Coventry are from the Scandinavian countries. They support the Sky Blues having seen them on TV (often back in the Premier League days), and wanting to support someone other than the big clubs, having a City replica shirt when a child or the all Sky Blue subbuteo team when they were youngsters.

One of the original SBI members Albi Mozer, from Switzerland, was a 'newspaper Arsenal supporter' and was at Highbury in 1975. They played Coventry and won 5-0. He became a Sky Blues supporter after the game because even after the 5th goal went in, the several hundred Coventry supporters in the corner of the ground continued singing whilst the rest of Highbury remained silent. Albi and his wife Andrea pictured below with

Barry and I are regular visitors to games.

CCLSC provide SBI members, when they are over in the UK and can get to a game, with a ticket collection service so they can sit with other CCLSC members at games. Several SBI members are

regular visitors, travelling over on one or two occasions each season and joining us for pre match drinks and at games.

CCLSC provides regular communication to its members. It issues a monthly e-newsletter, which features travel and ticketing information. The Newsletter was awarded the APFSCIL Newsletter of the Year Award in both 2017 and 2019. Our away match ticketing collection service enables CCLSC members to sit (stand) together at away games. It also issues a pub and directions email before each away game.

Organising group travel, in the period of 2012-20, has fallen on the shoulders of Simon Fahy, before his move to Canada, and in the later years to Adrian Hawthorne. We would all meet at Euston, before home games, or at other London mainline stations depending on where we were travelling that day. Simon would arrive with handfuls of printed train tickets. In recent years Adrian would have digital tickets. Both would regularly have to wait at the barrier for those members running late - Group travel meant we had to travel together! They know who they are. Ross Sauvage did seem to perfect the practice of travelling on a later train with a copy of his ticket having been sent to him by phone (before the days of digital tickets). Ross always seemed to be able to persuade the Train Manager to let him travel.

The cost of leaving London during peak times, and often being unable to get back home outside of central London afterwards, prohibits group travel for midweek games. Members either drive, stay with relatives, friends or in hotels to be able to attend.

The group travelling from London are met at the designated pub by other members who travelled from other parts of the country, not needing to travel through London, making their own way to the game.

In the eight years outside of the Championship, the regular group travellers from London to home games could be up to twenty or more. At the designated pubs we would often have 30 to 40. When visiting new grounds, during promotion seasons, or due to the 'protest' about watching home games outside of Coventry when some members only attending away games, we would see higher numbers. Up to 75-100 would gather at pubs in London, Milton Keynes and at the 'local' derby games at Walsall and Peterborough. Northern midweek games could see our numbers fall to single figures.

Match tickets for away games has been the domain of our "Man in the Midlands" Barry Chattaway. He has co-ordinated member requests to ensure wherever possible we were together in seating or terraces. Tickets were often collected at the designated pub as we didn't want Barry to be seen handing out tickets outside of grounds.

Selection of Pubs

CCLSC preference for pre match drinks is to visit pubs that serve real ale, food, are family friendly, and importantly that are away from the ground. In selecting pubs based on this policy the first port of call was to identify pubs in the Campaign for Real Ale (CAMRA) Good Beer Guide (GBG). Ideally they would be within a 20 to 30 minute walk from the ground, and not on the direct route from the railway station to the ground. Pubs closer to the ground often are designated home fans only or if a designated away fans pub, will often serve beers in plastic glasses. Where GBG pubs could not be easily identified, then contact with the local CAMRA branch has often identified suitable pubs.

We would generally only visit towns and cities once a season, and in some cases the visit might be years apart. By selecting our designated pub in the majority of cases from GBG pubs it gave some degree of certainty on beer condition. Local CAMRA members in those towns and cities had regularly visited those pubs and voted for their inclusion in the Good Beer Guide. Pubs can only be included in the Guide if the landlord or cellar manager has been in situ for at least 12 months.

Contacting pub landlords the week before our visit ensured that beers, staffing and food was available. Often when more than 20 members were anticipated the landlord would ask that food was pre ordered. We often had designated area set aside for us and pubs would open early to coincide with our train arrival times.

As a result of our selection policy, those pubs we visited that were not in the current Good Beer Guide often had beer ranges and quality that was acceptable, but when compared to Good Beer Guide pubs would be viewed in a different and sometimes less favourable light.

The wilderness years

Coventry City was relegated from the Championship in 2012 only returning for the 2020/21 season. The one season League One tour everyone expected didn't happen. We were to remain in the lower reaches of the English Football League for eight seasons. During that time CCLSC members travelled the length and breadth of the country following their team. We played home games in Coventry, Northampton and Birmingham, frequenting 4 designated 'home' pubs and we had away days at 71 different clubs (and went to Wembley) with CCLSC members attending 127 different designated pubs.

It was not always easy to watch the Sky Blues during these eight years. There were the lows of a further relegation in 2017, to the fourth tier of the Football League for the first time since 1959, and playing through this period not having a ground of our own. This was followed by the highs of two promotions and two successful Wembley appearances. In troubled times, as well as happy ones, there have been many occasions when the Sky Blue Army (SBA) and the players were one.

You cannot change your allegiance. Your team is your team – through good and bad. Long distance supporters often had to endure the taunts and jibes, from the armchair supporters of the "big" teams who were often their neighbours or workmates. This is especially so in London and the South East who seem to have as many Man United, Man City and Liverpool supporters as there are Arsenal, Chelsea, Tottenham, and West Ham fans, many of whom have only seen the inside of their team's grounds from their TV screen.

Many London and South East based members like me have long journey times, some of over an hour, just to get into London to catch the train to Coventry for home games. Some starts as early as 5.30 am have been required to get to those away games in the far north or west of the country. Even home games are away days!

I joined CCLSC in 1987 when I moved from Coventry to live in Kent and work in the other "City" (of London). I was a silent member for many years as I would drive with my family to home and away games. I was therefore not using either the travel or ticketing facilities provided by CCLSC. I would attend the Player and Officials Q&As, and eagerly looked forward to the magazine. At the CCLSC 35th Anniversary dinner, the lack of magazines, due to time and cost of printing, was discussed. I offered to produce an e-newsletter. I produced my first pub and directions email for the Yeovil away game in September 2012 and the last produced, due to the pandemic and the curtailment of the season, was for Ipswich away in March 2020. The exact period we were out of the Championship, playing in Leagues One and Two.

Everyone will have their own stories. This tells the story of a group of regular travellers, in those eight years. I have attempted to capture the magic of days out of CCLSC members following our beloved Coventry City home and away, so as to enjoy the socialising with friends who share the same passion for football, drinking and eating together in great pubs, visiting football grounds and even enjoying the delights of travelling on our rail network!. There is no substitute for the real thing, watching your team in grounds all around the country. We are all missing singing the Sky Blue Song together as one.

Each match day we spent together made memories that will last forever!

It does not detail the on-the-pitch exploits, except where they were relevant to the travelling support. It is more about the good and not so good pubs, the travel difficulties, the camaraderie and stories about our day out "often spoilt by the football". There were times when staying in the pub was seriously considered! I will leave the match by match analysis to the likes of Jim Brown and others.

These are the things currently lost, or seriously at risk, from the Covid-19 pandemic and they may never wholly be the same again.

Groundhog Day

It is Saturday morning in the football season. Coventry City is playing at home. Around London and the South East a dozen or so CCLSC members who are season ticket holders are leaving their homes between 8am and 9am to make their way into central London. They are making this first part of the journey on their own. Some have trains from their local station, which only has an hourly Saturday service into the major London stations like London Bridge, Victoria or Fenchurch Street. Some can walk, others have to catch a bus or get dropped off by family members at their local station. They must not miss that train.

Even when arriving into those mainline London stations, they still have another 20 minutes or so tube journey to get them to Euston.

The next part of the journey will be with friends and CCLSC members all travelling together. They all meet up at the Coffee Shop in the concourse at Euston Station. The talk is of the game to come, who should play, and perhaps their own journey that morning. Train disruptions and delays into London from Kent and Sussex are not unusual. Even those who can travel by tube from their homes to Euston often suffer delays.

Eyes are on the large boards that dominate Euston station. Is the 11.03 train on time? In recent years booking advanced tickets on Virgin (and more recently Avanti) trains meant that the group were allocated seats together. Had everyone travelling arrived?

The train platform is announced. No delays today. The group set off to board the train. They settle into their assigned seats and there is a combined sigh of relief. The fast train has its first stop at Rugby and then Coventry. It should arrive at 12.02.

If the train is running late, then a call to Barry Chattaway has to be made to let the pub know we are likely to be late. Barry will be in the pub before the London train group.

After Rugby, the allocation of taxis is the order of the day. Is anyone visiting relatives and perhaps being picked up at the station? Groups of four or five for the black cabs at Coventry station are assigned. A quick 5 minute taxi ride gets them to the designated home pub. There they will meet up with other CCLSC members at the pub. Those living outside of London and who didn't need to travel via Euston would arrive at different times. Food and drinks are consumed and at around 2.15 taxis are again assigned in groups of four or five and ordered.

The journey out to the Ricoh Arena would usually take around 15-20 minutes. Taxis drop their passengers at the entrance to the car park at the Arena. Unless that is you are travelling with Eric Whiting. He is able to persuade the security guards he is unable to walk that far and his taxi and fellow passengers are allow to drop off at the Casino entrance. The walk from there is significantly reduced.

We were a group of fanatical supporters who wanted to arrive at 2.55pm in jeans and replica shirts. It was not the prawn sandwich brigade for us.

For the games at the Ricoh after the match it was a quick dash through the large Tesco Superstore adjacent to the ground, to join the taxi rank queue. In the last couple of years however the trains did stop at the Ricoh and the 5 minute journey back to Coventry station was the preferred transport option.

After games at the Ricoh, we were usually back into Euston by 7 pm. Some went for another drink as they waited for their train home. Adrian and I would have tight connections from London Bridge (or have a 30-45 minute wait for our  next train) so as the train approached Euston we would say our goodbyes and walk through the train to the front. This hopefully gave us a few minutes head start to get to the tube. Early Saturday evening crowds would on occasions mean that we were still waiting for the next tube train when others arrived on the tube platform. No advantage gained.

The journey back to Euston was regularly delayed at Coventry. The Virgin train followed the slower stopping West Midlands train from Birmingham and as we stood on the platform the arrival time would slowly move backwards. That few minutes would cause further delays to those with connections in London.

The result that day would have a bearing on the journey. A win and the mood amongst the travelling group considerably improved. After a defeat or poor performance, the journey and probably the whole weekend would have a dampener put on it. The early years saw Coventry City near the bottom of League One and eventually relegated. It was this period that embodied the phrase 'a good day out spoilt by the football'.

If the one hours journey from Coventry was unbearable, just imagine those even longer journeys. Defeats at Plymouth, Rochdale and Scunthorpe tested the optimism and the friendship of the group. One of the longest journeys times was to Shrewsbury, with the very slow journey to and from Wolverhampton. We were never to win at Shrewsbury in this time.

Arrival back into London meant the return train journey out to Kent, Sussex or wherever. Having left home before 9 am we would get home 12 hours later (unless a drink in central London was deemed necessary).

For the last season, where we were playing at St Andrews the day was the same. But just one hour earlier. The group travelled on the 10.23 arriving into Coventry at 11.22 and then Birmingham at 11.42. Those leaving at Coventry were at the Gatehouse at 11.30 and those travelling on to Birmingham would walk to the Woodman and be outside as it opened at noon.

On alternate Saturdays it was the same but rather than meeting at Euston it would be Kings Cross, Liverpool Street, Paddington, Victoria, Waterloo or Marylebone stations depending on which part of the country we were travelling to that day. The times were often earlier as we would be leaving London before 9 am to get to the north or west of the country.

Each Saturday, it was the same again, and again, and again. Groundhog Day!

Our military operation did not always run smoothly. Trains were not always on time. There were delays, cancellations and bus replacements to take into account. On a number of occasions we had to make the dash from Euston to Marylebone Station to catch the train north. Changing at Leamington Spa, or if fortunate enough to be collected by friends or relatives at Warwick Parkway and driven to the pub.

There were times that games were cancelled as we sat at Euston. On one occasion, against Lincoln we were fortunate that the train we had advanced tickets for was also cancelled. We were able to get a refund of our tickets that time.

Coventry 'Home' grounds

In the period outside of the Championship, between 2012 and 2020, the Sky Blues were to play at three different "home" grounds, the Ricoh Arena, Sixfields and St. Andrews. For long distance supporters even home games were away games.

Ricoh Arena – Coventry

The Ricoh Arena was originally built as a replacement for Highfield Road. It is a 32,000 seater and was a state of the art stadium at the time. The stadium bowl features were not universally liked by everyone. When partially filled with crowds of nearer 10,000 it resulted in a lack of atmosphere. It was located on the outskirt of the Coventry near to the M6, and is surrounded by car parks which turn it into a ghost town on non match days. Despite being built next to a railway line trains were not allowed to stop when major events were on! It was only in the last couple of seasons that trains actually stopped at the station on match days.

Coventry City played their first game at the Ricoh on 20 August 2005 against Queens Park Rangers.

It was owned at that time by Arena Coventry Limited (ACL) with Coventry City as tenants. ACL was owned jointly by

Coventry City Council and the Higgs Charity. By 2012 there was the start of a dispute between the Club owners SISU and ACL. In November 2014 Wasps became the owners of the Ricoh. There are many others, like Simon Gilbert, in his book *Coventry City A Club Without a Home'* who have written about this sad saga that continues to this day. I will therefore not go into any great detail on this here.

The Sky Blues played at the Ricoh for the 2012-13 season. Coventry City went into administration and suffered a 10-point penalty as a consequence and when ACL refused to accept the CVA (Company Voluntary Agreement) proposed by the administrator, a second 10-point deduction the following season was applied by the Football League. The Sky Blues were to groundshare and play their fixtures in the 2013-14 season at the home of Northampton Town. An initial two year deal to bring the Sky Blues back to the Ricoh was agreed in 2014. They were to return on 21 August 2014 and the deal was extended meaning that the Sky Blues continued to play their home games at the Ricoh until the end of the 2018-19 season.

A number of CCLSC members had season tickets on the half way line of the East Stand. Others sat with their friends and families elsewhere in the stand. Except for one or two games only the East Stand and the two-tiered West Stand (Main Stand), with the Executive Boxes and Directors Box, were open to Coventry City supporters. The South Stand, behind the goal, was the away fans stand. The North Stand, renamed by Wasps the Alan Higgs Charity Stand, was often not open to supporters. Coventry fans were in both the South and North Stands for the near capacity games in the Area Final against Crewe and the second home coming against Gillingham.

Results
The home record was as follows

	Won	Drew	Lost
2012-2013	7	7	9
2014-2015	5	8	8 (first two at Sixfileds)
2015-2016	12	6	5
2016-2017	8	7	8
2017-2018	13	4	6
2018-2019	9	7	7

Sixfields Stadium – Northampton

In order to fulfil their fixtures in 2013-14 Coventry City were to play at Sixfields Stadium in Northampton. They were to play 35 miles from home in front of small crowds. Sixfields with a capacity of less than 8,000 had a two-tier main stand and two stands of similar size behind each goal. Opposite the main stand was a stand under construction.

Like many Sky Blues supporters CCLSC members were split. Some members were adamant they would not go if games were not played in Coventry, others wanted to go to show their support for the team, which to be honest, is the main reason for being involved in CCLSC as long distance supporters. If they were to go, it was for the team, not the owners, ACL or the Council, or whoever. "It's the team of young lads who everybody should be supporting", became a common theme amongst several members.

Those that did watch the team at Sixfields would mainly go in the Dave Bowen Stand behind the goal. There were one or two members who purchased season tickets in the Main Stand. On the grass banking behind the Dave Bowen Stand supporters would gather and protest about the Club playing at Northampton This was to become known as 'Jimmy's Hill'.

Results
2013-2014   won 9 drew 8 lost 6
2014-2015   won 1 drew 1 (other games at Ricoh)

St Andrews – Birmingham

Coventry City and Wasps' legal dispute continued and on 24 July 2019 the Club announced that it would groundshare at Birmingham City's St Andrew's Stadium for the 2019/20 season. The 29,000 capacity stadium was unlikely to be full, and crowds were reduced as a consequence of playing in Birmingham. The Spion Kop stand along the side of the pitch would be opened for Coventry City supporters.

The reasons for the groundshare seemed different this time to many supporters. There were around 30 CCLSC members who committed to season tickets and we arranged for these to be together in the same block. Others not able to travel regularly would buy tickets in this area when attending games.

The pitch at St Andrews was a factor often quoted as one of the reasons for the team only losing one home game that season. It was in fantastic condition despite being played on every week, and was a huge contrast to the playing surface at the Ricoh where the pitch was described by one member as being like a ploughed field after rugby had been played on it regularly. The groundshare continued for the 2020/21 season, although initially without the prospect of fans attending games because of the Covid-19 pandemic.

Results
2019-2020 won 11 drew 9 lost 1

And one more?

As this book was completed for publication the prospect of Coventry City having a new home ground was raised for the umpteenth time. News was issued that a brand new stadium would be built in partnership with Warwick University, on a site close to the student campus.

So. in future years CCLSC members' travel to games could take a new direction.

Coventry "home" pubs

In the period outside of the Championship, between 2012 and 2020, the Sky Blues were to play at three different "home" grounds, the Ricoh Arena, Sixfields and St. Andrews. For long distance supporters even home games were away days. During this same period CCLSC members had four "home" pubs. These were the Whitefriars, in Coventry, the Lamplighter in Northampton, the Gatehouse in Coventry (following the closure of the Whitefriars), and the Woodman in Birmingham.

The **Whitefriars Olde Ale House** had been the "home" of CCLSC for many years. This 14th century building was once part of the Whitefriars monastery, subsequently a butcher's shop before being renovated and made into a pub. The small front room used to be a kitchen used by the friars, with a welcoming fire in the winter months.

Jim Brown mentioned that at first a number of us were dubious as there seemed to be limited space but we quickly 'bought in' to the history and ambience of this old fashioned pub. There was no pretension and it somehow avoided the gentrification and faux history route many similar establishments went down.

By 2012, we no longer used the upstairs room. Some might remember the steep staircase and spilling their beers going up or nearly falling over coming down.

We have been regulars, before games, for many years and Matt, his Dad, Mary, Trish and the staff always gave us a warm welcome.

There were always good beers on tap, an ever changing range of ales, wonderfully kept by a caring if somewhat roguish landlord. There were always extra barrels ready just in case! He kindly offered a discount scheme which probably encouraged us to drink more than we might otherwise had done. His regular beers were from breweries like Jarl, Byatts and Holdens. The Plum Porter was a firm favourite of Charles Tomkins and Robin Ogleby.

My own preferred plan was to start with the lighter golden beers before proceeding onto the stronger darker beers. John Bryant (known as JB) would start with a cider before quickly moving onto red wine.

When the Club announced it was to play its home games at Northampton in the 2013-14 season CCLSC members, similar to all Coventry City supporters, were split over playing at Sixfields. Some went into the ground, some travelled to Northampton and stood on "Jimmy's Hill", whilst others boycotted "home" games altogether. As an organisation we made the decision that we would not provide group travel during this period, but individuals would make their own arrangements if necessary.

Chris Lambert (Lambo), who had been a committee member in the early years of CCLSC and by now living in Northampton, offered up some research on pubs that could be used.

There were three entries in the CAMRA Good Beer Guide that would meet our criteria. These were the Malt Shovel, the Wig & Pen and the Lamplighter (in the street where he lived). The first two were well patronised by Saints fans (Northampton Rugby) which could have been a problem if there was a fixture clash, but both were nearer Sixfields than the Lamp. All three had a good range of real ales, all did home-cooked food, and had beer garden facilities. The Wig also offers 10% discount for CAMRA members, and had Sky (but it was a rugby-oriented pub so we were not sure if they showed football).

We were to conclude that those going to the first game at Sixfields would meet at the **Lamplighter**. It was away from the ground, the town centre and the railway station. We never looked further and so it was to become our "home" for the time we were exiled.

It was perhaps the only positive from our time there. The beer range of well-kept beers, food and our welcome was the reason. It had one large room plus a small snug to the rear. It was to be the Local CAMRA Pub of the Year 2013. Several CCLSC members might well have added their vote that year.

Northampton is some 35 miles south of Coventry. For those travelling from London this may have been seen as an advantage. However, journey times from Euston were longer than to Coventry as trains stopped at several stations.

Many of the games at Sixfield were played on Sunday. So train travel was often disrupted by planned engineering works.

The Lamp did very good Sunday roasts, which were very popular with the locals. We had to book tables well in advance to ensure the football fans could be accommodated.

I can only recall one occasion where another teams' supporters visited the Lamplighter. A minibus full of Swindon supporters attended once, when a Beer Festival was on.

Lambo crossed the road from his home to join us at the Lamplighter before each game. He never did go to Sixfields himself. He would stay for a further pint as we all jumped in taxis or cars to go to the ground.

Maybe we knew something when we asked the barmaid to take a photo of us at the Sheffield United "home" game (above). It was to be the last Saturday game. Not that we missed going to Northampton, but we did miss the Lamplighter!

The long awaited return to the Ricoh finally arrived in September 2014. A crowd of over 27,000 turned up, despite the Gillingham game being moved to a Friday evening, being shown on Sky TV, and the difficulties of getting tickets.

That Gills game – what can be said?

After all the problems and issues getting tickets, all that was forgotten and what will be remembered will be the atmosphere, the noise as the team came out and the "Stand up if you love City" that went around the ground when Webster was down injured late in the second half, and of course, Ryan Haynes getting to the line to pull back for Frank Nouble's goal.

With the fantastic news that we are going home, Travel Secretary Simon Fahy looked again at travel arrangements for home games, starting immediately. Travel was booked weeks in advance.

The following week it was the first train trip to a home game, against Yeovil, for many months and another win. A dozen members made the trip, enjoying group travel from Euston for a £12 return rail fare. We were joined for the majority of the journey to Coventry by Tim Fisher, the Club Chairman, who came and sat with us and was willing to answer a wide ranging number of questions from the group. Our optimism about the Yeovil attendance was sadly misplaced. The majority thought it would be high teens or even over 20k. It was a disappointment therefore that only 11k turned up for the Yeovil game.

It was back to the **Whitefriars**, for our pre match drinks, before home games. We were to continue to visit before every home game from September 2014 until it closed in December 2016.

Members drifted into two distinct groupings. One group based themselves in the bar area and the other in the side room.

Honorary members Rod Dean and Jim Brown, and other long standing members like Geoff Moore, Mark Page, Don Chalk and Dave Long would squeeze themselves around a couple of tables in the bar area. Others who turned up from time to time, included Jonathan Strange, David Brassington, and Mike Cahill.

There were children too, Jim's son Alastair, Dave's girls, Esme and Ella, and Geoff's sons Andrew and Chris. The new generation of supporters were being introduced to the match day rituals!

The London train group would congregate in the side room. Regular travellers over these years would, amongst others, include Colin Henderson, John Bryant, Robin and George Ogleby, Charles Tomkins, Chris Webb, Simon Fahy, Rob Stevens, Adrian Hawthorne, Mick Adams and I.

The Whitefriars crowd was completed by Barry Chattaway and other regulars Alastair Laurie, Eric Whiting, John Burgess, and in the latter years Rod Williams, Kev Randall and Phil Higgins. The new generation included Matt Chattaway, Scott Harbertson, Christian Cation along with George Ogleby.

On a Saturday the London train usually arrived into Coventry at 12.02 so with taxis the group travellers were in the Whitefriars just after noon. Barry would arrive at 11.30pm on most match days, as a result of his own transport connections. Barry was always there in the side room, a beer and his little black book in hand, when everyone else arrived. In the winter months he would start the fire going, ensuring it was glowing by the time we arrived. As time went on Barry would only accept match ticket requests on-line and his famous black book bit the dust, instead holding court concentrating on match ticket distribution. Members arriving would ask where Barry was before what beers were on that day.

Folklore has it that Barry had a key to the Whitefriars. He had arrived on one occasion and as it was raining had been let in by the cleaner. It was suggested if he found the door wasn't open in future, he should knock and someone would let him in, even though the pub didn't open until noon. Without us knowing how, he was able to be in the pub early each match day.

Matt, the landlord, often turned up late if he had had a "busy" Friday night – and so it was just as well Barry had his own key to let us all in. This meant, however, that the ever dependable Mary (pictured with Barry below) would have to start serving behind the bar before she could crack on with the food.

There was a chalk blackboard sign outside the pub which stated that food was available on Saturday lunchtime ONLY when Coventry City played at home. Without the CCLSC members buying food and several pints of beer, or glasses of wine in John Bryant's case, it wasn't economical to offer food to what was essentially a student pub for the rest of the week.

Mary would often say she had to consult the fixture lists so she knew when she was going to be required to cook food on a Saturday. The Monster Breakfast for Robin and George Ogleby, and the sizzlers were very popular. Rob Parker is remembered for demolishing two steak sizzlers, one after the other on one occasion. Others like Jim Brown tended to stick to non-cooked food – their cheese and onion batches (rolls or baps for those not from Coventry) were delicious. There was a downside to the Whitefriars, the smell of burning fat from the kitchen.

Mary was temporarily replaced at one time by an Irish chef, who while managing to feed us well when sober, sadly went missing on the Saturday after St Patrick's night. Fortunately though, and for JB in particular, Matt said we could nip next door and bring in some kebabs.

At the end of each season Matt would provide a free lunch for the group as a thank you for the amount of trade we had given him during the previous season.

On one occasion in October 2014, Sandra Garlick, in her role as the Chair of the Stadium Forum, and wanting to meet supporters groups, joined a group of CCLSC members in the Whitefriars before the Crawley game. I think she was surprised about the large number of "London members" attending.

We never phoned for taxis to get us to the Ricoh, as there was always a steady stream passing the Whitefriars. There is a saying you can lead a horse to water but you can't make it drink. It felt like that trying to organise everyone into groups of five to get taxis out to the Ricoh. There was always someone who went to the toilet, just as their five was leaving. Barry of all people was left behind on one occasion.

We received devastating news just before Christmas 2016 that our other "home", the Whitefriars Olde Ale House, was to close, with immediate effect.

As Barry put it in his email notifying the committee members and regular travellers, "it feels like we are losing our football team and now we have lost our pub. A sad day indeed."

We had some great memories there. We always felt welcome whenever we had been there.

Those who had met in the main bar area at the Whitefriars moved to the Old Windmill, in Spon Street. This highly recommended pub is divided into a number of small rooms but only offered pub snacks. The pork pies came recommended.

Both these reasons were seen as restrictive given that many of the London travellers would have left home early and arrived home late on match days. Hot food was nearly as much a priority as good beers.

January 2017 saw the CCLSC regular travellers try out the **Gatehouse Tavern** before the home games against Bolton and Fleetwood. This followed extensive research by me with the local CAMRA branch and by colleagues living in the Coventry area.

The Gatehouse was rebuilt from the shell of the former Leigh Mills gatehouse. The garden is the largest within the city centre. Eric Whiting was impressed that Draught Bass was a regular beer. Up to six ever changing beers were on from the likes of Church End, Purity and Byatt's.

We were made very welcome on that first occasion by Martin, the Landlord, who kindly provided nugget and chips for the group on the New Year's Monday, when he realised we had travelled from London and the South East and he wasn't providing lunchtime meals that day. He also operated a beer discount scheme which to JB's horror didn't include wine. Martin rectified that and JB had probably the only wine discount card in existence.

The food selection available before that Fleetwood game went down well, as did the range of beers. This helped with the sadness of the closure of the Whitefriars. The Gatehouse food choice and beer range on offer was to be maintained going forward.

Martin would ensure food was served from 5pm for those evening games and was always served quickly on Saturday match days. The food menu favourites included lamb shanks, big breakfasts and gammon and chips.

We continued to be impressed with the Gatehouse and landlord Martin was presented, before the Scunthorpe game in August 2018, with our Pub of the Season Award 2017/18. As I said when presenting the award, "Martin and his staff consistently served a range of real ales in excellent condition and good food in a family friendly atmosphere throughout the season, which are all key criteria for CCLSC visits, and the Gatehouse thoroughly deserved the award".

Martin also continued with the tradition of providing at the last game of the season a drink "on the house".

We would be playing our "home" games at St Andrews, the home of Birmingham City for the 2019/20 season. We again recognised a wide range of views amongst our membership, from those who would attend away games only and not attend home games outside of Coventry, to those that would go to St Andrews.

At our AGM held in June, we confirmed and agreed our policies on membership, travel and ticketing for the coming season. In particular, Travel Secretary, Adrian Hawthorne, said he was prepared to book train tickets via Coventry or direct to Birmingham depending on members' wishes.

Some of the regular rail travellers from London wanted to continue to support local businesses and taxis and agreed, despite a slight increase in travel time and costs that they would go via Coventry. This was initially for the first few games whilst reviewing alternative options nearer the ground in Birmingham. They broke their journey at Coventry, and continue to meet at the Gatehouse Tavern for pre match lunch and drinks, before continuing onto Birmingham. Travel was on earlier trains and Martin at the Gatehouse agreed to serve food earlier to facilitate us. A few members, including John Bryant and Adrian Hawthorne, left the train at Coventry, throughout the season. JB would join Phil, Eric, Kev and Barry who continued to meet at the Gatehouse regularly before games. They were joined by others depending upon journey times.

Travel to St Andrews was not as bad as many expected. Whilst some members continued breaking their journey at Coventry, to continue meeting at the Gatehouse, others travelled direct to Birmingham where the **Woodman** quickly became the preferred pub. Members found they used a combination of bus, taxi and walking, to and from the pub and ground. Regulars from the London train with me that season included, Colin

 Henderson, Rob Stevens, Charles Tomkins, Chris Webb, Robin and George Ogleby. We were joined at the Woodman by Alastair Laurie, Rod Williams, John Burgess, Martin Spare and Jim McIlwaine amongst others. Jim, not a regular attendee at the Whitefriars or Gatehouse, preferring to drink closer to the Ricoh, was the member who attended the most away games during the period we were out of the Championship.

Rob Stevens, Colin Henderson and a few others gave me feedback after a research trip in early August to find our "new" home pub. They visited several pubs touring around the Digbeth and Central Birmingham area.

The short version was that Robin Ogleby came out after getting his second pint at the Woodman and declared "This is the one. This is the Birmingham Gatehouse". Considering how many pubs our esteemed Competitions Secretary visits in the average month, surely this was recommendation enough.

The Woodman is a two roomed restored Victorian pub adjacent to the HS2 station building works. This makes it look isolated as you walk through Eastside park which is popular with skateboarders. It has several restored features, including a glided and etched mirror in the centre of the bar. For those in the smaller back room beers were served through a small hatch from the main bar.

It served Castle Rock beers regularly along with two or three guest ales sourced from national breweries. Hearty food was available.

Rob Steven's organised a "Balti Brunch" on one occasion (pictured) when food wasn't available. That lunch was almost wrecked when the delivery driver had no idea how to get to the Woodman.

We were always made very welcome at the Woodman, even when we were to play Birmingham City in the FA Cup.

The CCLSC Tour of 2012-2020

This is a collection of fascinating insights into real supporters, passionately watching real football at some of the not so glamorous grounds, whilst visiting some of the best pubs around the country. These stories of our trips to the away grounds visited are grouped in alphabetical order.

In this period we were to play at four Premier League stadiums. Two had been built since Coventry had been in the Premier League, the Arsenal Emirates and the Amex at Brighton. Tottenham's White Hart Lane, the scene of two great Premier League relegation escapes, had fond memories for the older CCLSC members. Since our visit in 2013 it has been demolished and a new ground built on the same site. The fourth was to the much redeveloped Vicarage Road at Watford.

There was a lot of curiosity with the visits to grounds we had not played at before. This increased the numbers travelling.

In 2012-13 we played at seven grounds for the first time: Yeovil, Stevenage, MK Dons, Crawley and Dagenham & Redbridge. In addition we visited the new grounds of Shrewsbury and Colchester. The following season the FA Cup game was the first visit to AFC Wimbledon's ground in Kingston and, before that season, we had not appeared at Sixfields. In 2015 there were visits to the new Chesterfield stadium and Fleetwood and in 2016 we visited Burton. Oxford's Kassam Stadium, Bristol Rovers' Memorial Park and the New Wembley were all new grounds in 2017. There were five new grounds in 2017-18: Barnet, Accrington Stanley, Forest Green, Newport and Cheltenham.

Sadly, by the 2020/21 season, seven of the Clubs and grounds visited were no longer in the EFL (English Football League). These are Barnet, Chesterfield, Dagenham & Redbridge, Hartlepool United, Notts County, Yeovil Town and York City. Even sadder is that Bury who we visited on three occasions have gone out of existence.

We also had several members attend pre season friendly matches at Sutton United and played Portsmouth at Havant & Waterlooville and Watford at Boreham Wood.

We were to play at Wembley twice, winning the Checkatrade Trophy in 2017 and the League Two Play-Off Final in 2018.

In the following pages are some of the memories of the CCLSC visits to those Clubs, grounds and pubs we visited following Coventry City.

Accrington Stanley
Ground – Wham Stadium (known by many as the Crown Ground)

A small ground holding just over 5,400, set in a picturesque area, with views over the fields and hills behind the Coppice Terrace (pictured) where the majority of the Sky Blue Army were standing. It is an open terrace so the SBA needed to be especially loud for their singing to carry around the ground. Those who were in the covered seating area did complain about the lack of space between the rows of seats.

Results
14 Oct 2017   0-1   League Two
02 Mar 2019   1-0   League One   (Enobakhare)

Pub

We visited the **Peel Park Hotel** on both of our trips to Accrington. It is opposite the site of the original Accrington Stanley ground. They served a range of beers from local breweries and the northern staple of pie and peas. I was not able to go to our first ever visit in October 2017, due to grandson duties (the only away match I missed that season I recall). I had contacted the pub, beforehand as usual, giving them notice that there would be around fifty or so members arriving. The group duly arrived just after noon, having walked the 20 minutes or so from the station through what can only be described as typical northern terraced housing. The landlady and her daughter were the only staff on and they had little food available.

Robin Ogleby rang me to say that the landlady didn't know we were planning on meeting at the Peel. You only had one job was the tone of the call! I was put onto the Landlady and explained that I had indeed called on the Friday the week before and spoken to a man; giving the numbers attending and that we required hot food. There was a long silent pause on the other end of the phone..... . her son had passed on the wrong message she said as she had extra staff, beer and food on last Saturday, when Luton played. He was going to "get a good spanking" we were told. The Peel had been disappointed with the near total lack of away (Luton) supporters at the pub given the phone call and son's message.

Everyone at the Peel that day said the Landlady and her daughter were magnificent keeping beer and food orders coming. I subsequently sent a message on their Facebook page thanking them for looking after us. They were pretty old school they said and didn't have email.

On our subsequent visit in March 2019, I ensured that the landlady herself was contacted and we were well looked after.

That game was won by a solo effort by Bright Enobakhare, a fans favourite on loan from Wolves, who dribbled through the defence before slotting the ball into the corner of the net.

The scheduled away game at Accrington in March 2020 didn't take place due to the curtailment of the season. CCLSC had purchased 37 match tickets for the match. Pictured are Sarah and her Dad Kevin and Richard, Leslie and Charlie.

AFC Wimbledon
Ground – Cherry Red Records Stadium (originally the KingsMeadow Stadium)

This small and tidy ground has a capacity of only 4,850. The Sky Blue Army were located mostly on the side of the pitch in the Rygas Stand. This small shallow terrace is partly covered to the rear and can accommodate up to 725 visiting fans. We were also allocated a small number of seats behind the goal.

Surprisingly the team dugouts are not located in front of the Main Stand, but opposite in front of the Rygas Stand, which leads to a procession of players and club officials across the pitch, at half time and at full time.

Results

Date	Score	Competition	Scorers
08 Nov 2013	3-1	FA Cup	(Wilson, Baker, og)
14 Feb 2017	1-1	League One	(Jones)
11 Aug 2018	0-0	League One	

We were denied a visit to a hostelry for the last day of the season in 2020 because the season had been curtailed due to the Covid-19 pandemic. We had planned a return to the Albion again after a successful visit in 2018. We had changed pubs for each of our previous visits in this period and with AFC Wimbledon going home it would be our final visit to KingsMeadow.

Pub

In November 2013, we played on a Friday evening in the FA Cup and visited **Woodies**, in New Malvern, a free house that had its walls and ceiling festooned with a treasure trove of sporting memorabilia, pictured below.

The CCLSC members were huddled along the Cow Shed side of the ground and all had tales to tell of getting lost, taking the wrong train or were just caught in traffic. The start of the game was delayed 15 minutes due to the Friday evening traffic chaos in SW London. The AFC Wimbledon keeper, who was stuck in traffic, failed to make the start of the game. His replacement made a horrendous error to gift Callum Wilson the equaliser. We eventually won 3-1.

We had taxi issues from Woodies that night. The four minibuses arrived on time to take us to the ground. What I could not understand was why we had 3 members left standing. Tim Ward, who lived locally, arranged for Mrs Ward to drive the last few members to the ground.

A number of members had shown their initiative when it looked like tickets would not be available on general sale. They used their London and Home Counties addresses to obtain tickets in the "home" end. Several were then able to gain admission into the away area, thanks to helpful stewards, whilst others had a different story and had to repress their celebrations.

On our next visit in February 2017, it was another evening match, this time midweek. Woodies was deemed too far from the ground and we moved to the Antelope, in Surbiton. **The Antelope** served 10 changing beers, mainly from independent breweries and micros,

including a regular stout and porter. It was the CAMRA Branch Pub of the Year for 2016. It was only 400m from Surbiton station, which was a much easier journey from central London. Taxis were still required to get to the ground.

We eventually got to play on a Saturday in August 2018, for the first match of the season. **The Albion**, in Kingston was a 20 minute walk from the ground, so no taxis were needed unlike for the Antelope for our previous midweek visit.

The Albion served up to 10 different ales, with home cooked food and had a large patio.

Upon arrival we were impressed that all the tables had been set out for Coventry supporters throughout the pub. The pub was extremely busy that day as the Leamington & Warwick Supporters Club coach also turned up. The owner did think we were the same group of supporters!

Colin Henderson, pictured, had his two brothers over from Australia.

Arsenal
Ground – Emirates Stadium

The Emirates holds over 60,000 and away fans are usually housed in the lower tier corner of the South East Stand. With the very large Sky Blue allocation the Sky Blue Army were given the away area, which holds 3,000 and in addition the area behind the goal and upper tiers to accommodate the 8,000 and 5,000 plus attending our two visits.

Whilst it was our first visit to the Emirates in 2012 it proved a disappointing experience for many. There was excessive policing and a lack of facilities given to the Sky Blues supporters in the lower tier that evening. Interestingly, the two pitch invaders came from the Arsenal end!

One steward confirmed that on police instructions all Coventry fans were to be searched upon entry. Clearly this had not been communicated (unlike for the Olympics at the City Of Coventry Stadium – the Ricoh) resulting in hundreds, if not thousands of Sky Blues supporters still outside when the game kicked off. Arsenal fans on the same train as me going back to Kent that evening confirmed they had not been searched on entry.

There were limited toilet facilities available for the many supporters in the huge block 24 behind the goal. A steward, attempting to placate supporters, said this was because we had been given additional seating in what was normally a home supporters section. Large toilet facilities reserved for this area were closed off by iron gates. The steward added this was always the same problem when away teams were allocated this area.

Results
26 Sep 2012   1-6   League Cup   (Ball)
24 Jan 2014   0-4   FA Cup

Pub

We were drawn against Arsenal in cup competitions in 2012 and again in 2014. Several thousand Sky Blues supporters went to the Emirates on each of these occasions. The

 **Compton Arms** was an old favourite of CCLSC members when visiting Highbury in the Premier League days. By popular demand we returned to this back street village-like pub, with its simple furnishing and unpretentious low ceilings serving Greene King ales. The outside area on the cobbled stone road was extremely busy on both occasions.

We had been beaten 6-1 in the Capital Cup on our first visit but in the second game in 2014 both the team and the SBA gave a good account of themselves. The final score, a 4-0 defeat, probably flattered the Gunners. Arsene Wenger sent out his stars, including Ozil, the Ox and his strongest defence against our battling League One team.

Much of the press and TV attention was on the Club's situation. The 'Why and What' protest was given a lot of coverage by BT Sport and even applauded by the Arsenal fans.

The SBA singing *Twist and Shout* went viral on YouTube that evening. My personal favourite song that night was, when the floodlights temporarily failed and the Arsenal fans used their phones for light, the SBA singing "we are Coventry City, we play in the dark".

A couple of interesting facts caught my eye in February 2014. The Sky Blues playing budget that season was around £2m but the Manchester City's wage bill for 2012/13 was a staggering £233m. We all paid £25.50 for our match tickets at the Emirates. Liverpool fans paid £62 in the next round of the FA Cup to "stand" in the same seats.

Barnet
Ground – Hive Stadium

Copyright Gavin Black

The Hive Stadium was opened in 2013, and has a capacity of 6,500. It was originally envisaged as the site for a new ground for Wealdstone FC, but with their financial difficulties Barnet took over the project. It is located just less than six miles from their old Underhill ground. The Sky Blue Army were housed in the North Stand (pictured). This modern stand had no supporting pillars and good facilities.

Results
07 Oct 2017   0-0   League Two

From the Cannons Park tube station, which is on the Jubilee line it was a 10 minute walk to the away entrance through a set of playing fields, with views in the distance of the Wembley Arch.

The large away supporters bar located behind the stand was well received by members. This spacious bar area had large TV screens. One downside is that beers like at other grounds are sold in plastic glasses.

Pub

Our one league appearance at the Hive was in October 2017, a disappointing 0-0 draw. The match was shown on Sky TV and the kick off moved to 12.30. The area around Barnet's new ground is, shall we say, devoid of real ale pubs, or indeed pubs! The early kick off didn't help those collecting match tickets or wanting an early pre match beer (or two). Most members travelling through central London to the game had to pass through Baker Street, so for location and not for beer reasons, we met at the **Metropolitan Bar** by Baker Street tube. It was not up to our usual standard, and several members had to return beers. To be fair to the pub and the staff, these were replaced without any problems, blaming the busy Friday evening for beers running out.

Barnsley
Ground - Oakwell

This is a modern ground, with good facilities which has a capacity of just over 23,000. The Sky Blue Army were in the North Stand at one end of the ground in the cantilevered stand with its good acoustics.

Results
04 Jan 2014	2-1	FA Cup	(Moussa, Clarke)
03 Mar 2015	0-1	League One	
01 Mar 2016	0-2	League One	
30 Mar 2019	2-2	League One	(Hiwala, Thomas)

Pub

Our (then) new policy of calling ahead to advise the landlord of approximately how many would be joining us for that pre-match drink was certainly working before the FA Cup game in January 2014. We spoke to the landlord at the **Old No 7,** who mentioned that pub got very crowded on match days.

The landlord was a Blackpool fan and encouraged away supporters. When I mentioned that there may be more than twenty of our members attending he offered to open the downstairs  vault cellar bar just for us. The Acorn beers were in excellent condition and we were allowed to bring in food from the nearby Greggs. Jim O'Brien scored for Barnsley but a last minute Leon Clarke goal put the Sky Blues into the next round.

Adrian Jeffrey and Stuart Nicholson are based in Wakefield and Leeds but they regularly join us at northern games.

We returned for an evening kick off league match in March 2015 and March 2016 to a full pub. The downstairs bar, we were informed, only opened on a Friday and Saturday (or when we contacted them beforehand!).

For our latest visit, in March 2019, a number of regular travellers, including myself, were invited to join owners of a local firm in the hospitality suites. There were several jokes about members having to drink lager due to the lack of any real ale.

The lack of food at Old No 7 meant that several members met initially at the nearby **Silkstone Inn**. This Wetherspoons pub has a coal theme (the Silkstone Seam stretched under Barnsley) and serves two regular beers and three guest beers along with the usual comprehensive hot food range. There was some confusion that day as members who were collecting match tickets, turning up at the Old No 7, and then going to the wrong Spoons, before eventually finding Barry and their tickets.

Birmingham City
Ground – St Andrew's Tillion Trophy Stadium

St Andrews has a capacity of 29,000. Apart from the Main Stand the rest of the stadium is modern. The Sky Blue Army were in the Gil Merrick Stand, pictured, for our 'away' game.

Result
04 Feb 2020   2-2   FA Cup   (Bakayoko, Biamou)

Pub

The FA Cup game in 2020 against Birmingham was of course, very unusual. You couldn't make it up! We played the "home" game, at their home, St Andrews. The replay meant we were the "away" team in the away end. **The Woodman,** which had become our "home" pub when playing at St Andrews had both sets of supporters mixing, with the Woodman's beer range and food being enjoyed along with the banter. We were beaten on penalties after conceding in added time at the end of 90 minutes and again at the death in extra time. Over the two games many believed it was the Sky Blues who played the football against our landlords and the Championship side.

Blackpool
Ground – Bloomfield Road

It has modern stands on three sides and a capacity of just over 17,000. The 3,200 plus City fans in March 2016 were housed in the Stan Mortensen (North) Stand, at one end of the ground and in the East Stand. There were high expectations for the game that promotion could be achieved that season. We won and were 7th after the game. The pitch was probably one of the worst seen for some time. There was more sand on the pitch that on the beach!

Results
12 Mar 2016   1-0   League One   (Fortune)
21 Aug 2018   0-2   League One

Pub

Blackpool has seen the high and lows of pubs in the last few years.

We enjoyed a very successful visit to the **Bloomfield Brewhouse** in March 2016 when it had offered up to 8 cask ales. This included their own signature ale Ansdell 47 Blonde Ale, which was brewed on site, together with a range of craft beers and ciders.

It was all smiles as our large group arrived at Bloomfield Road. (L to R) Colin, Charles, Jim and Lambo.

This was despite the very large queues at the turnstiles. Blackpool fans were protesting about their owners and not attending. The game was deemed to be high risk. Everyone was being searched before entering the stadium.

The crowd that day was officially 8,869. With 3,200 Coventry City supporters most of our members in the ground thought the attendance was nearer 4,000 in total. Blackpool presumably counted season and advanced ticket sales.

In August 2018 an evening fixture reduced the numbers travelling. Many who made the trip stayed over. Those arriving early met at the **Pump and Truncheon**, in the centre, during the afternoon. Their beers confirmed their CAMRA Good Beer Guide status. Unfortunately, our designated pub near the ground, the Bloomfield Brewhouse, proved to be a big disappointment this time. The advertised cask ales were not on sale and whilst the landlord put on a couple of beers after we arrived, they were not ready and undrinkable. The weak excuse that they didn't sell enough real ale in midweek didn't help.

John and Janet Chamberlain (right) pictured below at the Bloomfield Brewhouse.

A promotion party had long been planned for April 2020, with "everyone" seemingly going. Hotels and B&Bs had been booked well in advance. The curtailment of the season meant it didn't happen.

Bolton Wanderers
Ground – University of Bolton Stadium

The stadium, with its capacity 28,700, can be seen from miles around. It is near the Middlebrook Retail Park. It suffers, like the Ricoh, from being out of town meaning fans mainly have to drive and park in large car parks at the stadium. The nearest train station is Horwich, a few minutes walk from the stadium. The Sky Blue Army were in the South Stand but the first few rows of the lower tier are not covered. The large contingent in August 2019 was in good voice.

Results
22 Nov 2016   0-1   League One
10 Aug 2019   0-0   League One

Pub

Our first visit to Bolton for many years was an evening fixture in November 2016. In accordance with our evening match policy, those few members who made the trip, met at the **Bee Hive**, near the stadium. The large Fayre & Square (Greene King) pub served IPA and Robinson's.

Our only other visit nearly didn't take place. In August 2019, Bolton were only able to confirm that the game would go ahead the day before. We therefore belatedly asked Rob, the Manager at the Wetherspoon **Spinning Mule**, in the town centre, if they would

accept a large group of "mature" CAMRA members who were also Coventry City supporters from London. He reserved the snug area for us. The Spinning Mule is named after Samuel Crompton's Mule revolutionary invention in cotton spinning that made Bolton famous. The Mule was in the CAMRA Good Beer Guide in 2019 and served 7 guest beers and the usual Spoons food.

That day we met up with Alan Rudderham (left with Barry and Val) at the Spinning Mule. He was to become our first SBI member from Kathmandu. The majority of the group walked back to Bolton railway station to catch the train for the short journey to Horwich.

Bolton played their youngest ever team that day. The off the field issues at Bolton meant they didn't have a single senior player available but managed a 0-0 draw. How we didn't win, by several goals, many on the way home could not understand.

Bournemouth
Ground – Vitality Stadium (known as Dean Court)

When we visited the Ted MacDougall Stand at the south end of the ground was not completed. The stadium back then had an open end. The ground is small only having a capacity of just over 11,300. The Sky Blue Army were located on one side of the East Stand, which is situated at one side of the pitch.

Result
26 Feb 2013   2-0   League One   (Clarke, Baker)

Pub

We have fond memories of the **Cricketers Arms,** which is conveniently situated between Bournemouth Central station and the ground. It is Bournemouth's oldest pub and its star attraction (apart from the CAMRA recognised beer) is the lounge.

This vaulted stable was once the boxing gym for none other than Freddie Mills, the former world champion.

We were to only visit Bournemouth once during this period, an evening fixture in February 2013. The game became notorious for the SBAs chant of "we thought you were dead" when David Bell came on as a second half substitute, after a long absence from the team.

Bournemouth were on their way to the Championship that season and subsequently the Premier League. It was a satisfying 2-0 win. Carl and John pictured.

Bradford City
Ground – Valley Parade (it was renamed the Utilita Energy Stadium in 2019)

Valley Parade underwent a number of changes since the fire in 1985 that claimed 56 lives. It has the huge Kop End, a modern two-tiered stand which combined with the two-tiered Main Stand holds an impressive 19,000, out of the overall capacity of 25,000. The rest of the ground looks a little out of place. The TL Dallas stand, also two-tiered, where the Sky Blue Army were behind one of the goals (pictured) has the upper tier overhanging the lower tier. Although for the evening October 2018 visit the reduced away following was housed in the East Stand.

Results

17 Nov 2013	3-3	League One	(Webster, Clarke, Wilson)
09 Aug 2014	2-3	League One	(Johnson 2)
24 Nov 2015	0-0	League One	
20 Aug 2016	1-3	League One	(Agyei)
23 Oct 2018	4-2	League One	(Clarke-Harris, Chaplin, Hiwala, Bayliss)

Pub

The pub of choice when visiting Bradford over the years has been the **Corn Dolly**. Near to the Forster Square station this CAMRA award winning pub has been consistent in its welcome of CCLSC members. The only food available is the traditional Yorkshire lunch of pie and peas.

A small group saw the 3-3 draw in November 2013. We were two up in 7 minutes before conceding a last minute penalty.

Sky Blue International (SBI) member Jorn Erik Larsen from Oslo, joined us on the long train journey from St Pancras to Bradford for the opening game of the 2014/15 season. According to his tweet he enjoyed his day with us where we introduced him to our English real ale. He was up for sampling pints of Keighley brewed Timothy Taylor Boltmaker, Burnley's Moorhouse, Pride and Pendle and the West Yorkshire brewed

Elland, Beyond the Pale. He drew the line at the Corn Dolly's pork pie and mushy peas for lunch, despite being informed it was a Yorkshire specialty, going instead for the more Norwegian and familiar McDonald's on the way to the ground.

Another midweek game in November 2015 saw no organised travel but a small group returned to the Corn Dolly.

By August 2016 we were well aware that it was only pie and peas at the Corn Dolly. Changing at Leeds, on the way up, several members purchased sandwiches etc to keep them going. There was a lack of toilets and food in the away end at Valley Parade. Perhaps only the old Colchester Layer Road and Portsmouth had worse toilets! See group photo from the Corn Dolly.

One of the more interesting discussions the travelling group had was on the train back from the August 2016 game. We were joined on the Leeds to Kings Cross train by Tim Fisher and sitting next to us was a Texan based businessman, who turned out to be Gareth Roberts, the Chairman and owner of Vanarama National League North football team, Bradford Park Avenue. Gareth Roberts explained that he didn't know yet whether Bradford Park Avenue could remain at their long-term home but he had been talking to the Bradford Council, who owned the site, to see what options were available. If not, he said they were prepared to relocate and build on another site. This sounded to us very familiar.

Gareth and Tim discussed their stadium ownership issues, match day and non-match day revenue generation and as one member commented, it took Mr Roberts only a few minutes to grasp the CCFC situation and the challenge. This was something that had taken many fans months to understand, if they understood it at all. If we had known how wealthy Roberts was, we might have tried to broker a deal (sic).

I met Steve Pittam, from Dubai, for the first time that day and chatted in the ground. He was to become a regular visitor over

the years, joining us at both pubs and at games. He would often take in several games on each trip. Although his record "coming home" in the 2018/19 season was that in the 8 away games he attended we drew two and lost the other six! To be fair to Steve, he did see us win at home that season on a couple of occasions. Steve is pictured in the sky blue T shirt at Wembley.

For our last visit in October 2018, it was a Wetherspoon steak at **Turls Green** for those arriving into Bradford on the Tuesday afternoon, before moving onto the Corn Dolly for our pre match drinks. It was good to see several "northern" based supporters join us at the Dolly.

Not many members travelling that day would have remembered the last time we had won at Bradford, back in 1959. Records are there to be broken.

For those, like me, staying over in Bradford that evening, celebrations continued back at the Turls Green, after the 4-2 win.

Brentford
Ground – Griffin Park

In 2012 and 2014 Griffin Park, with a 12,700 capacity, had seen better days and Brentford were back then planning on building a new ground at Lionel Road. They finally moved at the start of the 2020/21 season. The Sky Blue Army were in the small two tier stand with seating above and terracing below (pictured). As you would expect from an older ground the leg room was tight in the upper tier and the view obscured by pillars in the lower terrace.

Results
23 Oct 2012   1-2   League One   (McGoldrick)
22 Mar 2014   1-3   League One   (Wilson)

Pub

For the evening fixture in October 2012 at Brentford, despite Griffin Park then reputedly having a pub on all four corners of the ground (the *Griffin*, the *New Inn*, the *Royal Oak* and the *Princess Royal*) the suggested pub was the **Magpie & Crown**, in the High Street, which usually had up to 6 real ales, and is a few minutes' walk down the High Street away from the ground. It is a 10 minute walk from Brentford station.

We included the following in our newsletter at the time – "For those members interested in the "four corners of

Brentford", only the *Princess Royal* is genuinely on the corner of the ground. The *Royal Oak*, which is a locals pub that you might only wish to visit to complete the four, is on the same street block. The *New Inn* and the *Griffin* are on the opposite side of the street to the ground on New Road and Braemar Road respectively. The *Griffin*, a Fullers pub, serves real ale but does get busy. The *Princess Royal* and *New Inn* both have limited real ale, mostly lager and Guinness. The *New Inn* is the most popular historically with away fans. I can report that members Ross Sauvage, Dave Clare and Chris Webb were amongst those who completed the "Brentford 4" before the Brentford game that evening.

For our last visit in March 2014, Tam the landlady at the Magpie & Crown, put on extra staff when I said there would be up to 50 members joining us with the majority wanting food, with many pre ordering food. Most made the pub despite the major rail disruption experienced in getting from central London that Saturday lunchtime. The number was lower than normal as several regulars went to Stamford Bridge beforehand to try and get supporters from both Chelsea and Arsenal to sign the petition highlighting our Club's plight.hat time.

Brighton & Hove Albion
Ground – American Express Community Stadium

Copyright Paul Hazlewood

The 30,000 capacity Amex Stadium built out of town at Falmer, is an impressive sight as you drive passed on the A27. As you would expect from a new stadium the views are good. Although those in the first few rows did comment that they were looking at the feet of the players, being so low. The concourse is wide and the Club offer a real ale, usually from the visiting teams own area. The away end, in the corner of the South Stand, usually accommodates around 3,000 but for the FA Cup game, the 4,500 strong Sky Blue Army were given the complete South Stand.

Result
17 Feb 2018   1-3   FA Cup   (Clarke-Harris)

We met Premier League side Brighton in the 5th Round of the FA Cup in February 2018. With the advice to leave central Brighton early for the out of town Falmer based stadium, we had a pub dilemma before the Brighton cup tie.

Many had previously visited Brighton and saw games at both the Goldstone Ground and the Withdean Stadium. The AMEX was a new ground for many.

Pub

Thanks to Brighton based member, Rob Stevens, the **Brighton Beer Dispensary** (BBD) opened an hour early for us, at 11 am, and with pre ordered food members were fed and watered in good time to catch the "free" trains out to the ground.

The main front bar at the BBD had 9 handpumps with 3 dispensing ciders. They had their usual two real ales from Brighton Bier Co and two from Southey. It also had 9 keg fonts. The food offering was from local company Dizzy Gull.

Our estimate of members joining us at the BBD was somewhat under stated, much to the delight of landlords Jim and Cody. We organised with Jim and Jody food for 30 members. There were an estimated 75-100 who turned up on the day

Bristol City
Ground – Ashton Gate

Ashton Gate is both the home of Bristol City Football Club and from the 2014/15 season, Bristol Rugby Club. Work was then underway to transform Ashton Gate into a state-of-the-art 27,000 capacity stadium when we visited in 2014 and 2015.

Sky Blue fans were behind the goal, as for the JPT game earlier in the season, in the Aryeo Stand which gave better views, than on previous visits, where we were in the corner of the old Wedlock Stand.

With the stand at the far end of the pitch having been demolished the SBA took great delight in ridiculing the individual who could be seen standing on his garden shed roof watching the game.

Results
04 Feb 2014   2-1   League One   (Moussa, Webster)
10 Dec 2014   0-2   Johnstones Paint
18 Aug 2015   0-0   League One

Pub

In February 2014, an evening match meant only half a dozen members made it due to the difficulty of getting back into London and the South East after the game. The planned London tube strike didn't help.

It was a return to the **Merchant Arms**, a pleasant 20-25 minute walk to the ground. It was however a taxi ride from

Bristol Temple Meads station. It had become a favourite drinking establishment over the years on our previous visits. It was now a free house, after being one of the earliest Bath Ales tied houses, but still served two Bath beers.

We were to return to the Merchant Arms for the JPT Area Semi Final in December 2014 (pictured below).

Our last visit, this time on a Saturday, was in April 2015. That day we spoilt Bristol's promotion party, and if anything we were the better side on the day. The Sky Blue Army's applause near the end of the game to recognise Bristol's achievement was appreciated.

Club Historian and CCLSC Honorary member Jim Brown reported after the Bristol game that this was the first time that the Sky Blues have had four consecutive clean sheets away from home in league games.

Bristol Rovers
Ground – Memorial Stadium

Originally the home of Bristol Rugby Club the ground has a capacity of 12,300. It has a number of odd looking stands. One only runs for part of the pitch and has several supporting pillars. It is affectionately known by the 'Gas' fans as 'the Tent'. The Sky Blue Army were in the uncovered visitors terrace or seated behind the goal in the South Stand (pictured).

The Rovers fans are nicknamed 'gasheads'. This term comes from where the old Eastville stadium in Bristol was sited. Next to a (sometimes smelly) gas works!

Results

26 Dec 2016	1-4	League One	(Willis)
22 Sep 2018	1-3	League One	(Hyam)
05 Jan 2020	2-2	FA Cup	(Walsh, Craig (og))
01 Feb 2020	2-1	League One	(Allen, Walsh)

With no trains on Boxing Day 2016, the numbers travelling were reduced. Bristol based member Phil Smith had arranged with the landlord at the Victoria at Westbury-on-Trym, to expect our group for pre match drinks.

Pub

Upon arrival we found a notice on the door saying the pub wasn't opening until 6pm. We hastily decamped to the **Mouse**, just around the corner, where we were very well looked after. The Victoria's loss that day was the Mouse's gain, as around 25 members joined us, pictured below.

We have subsequently met at the **Post Office Tavern**, also in Westbury-on-Trym for our subsequent visits in September 2018 and our two visits in January and February 2020. Whilst the POT is over 1.7 miles from the ground, many of the pubs nearer did not meet our pub criteria.

Phil Smith ensured that the POT was open and ready for us when we arrived. An area had been set aside for us and we were very well looked after.

Our first visit was somewhat tainted by the taxis not all arriving to take us to the ground. Some arrived after kick-off and missed what was one of the worst first 10 minutes we played for many a season.

The weather that day was awful but Julie, Mary and Jane (pictured) had come prepared for the open terrace!

We have always enjoyed the range of beers on offer at the POT and the pre ordered food (a Sunday roast on one occasion). The Bass, served direct from the barrel, is stored in the back room but it is well worth asking for.

For the final visit we were joined by Jorg Nannestad and Gunner Glendrange on the train journey from Paddington. They were to display their fantastic Scandinavian Supporters Club flag both in the pub and at the ground.

Jorg was to present Barry, Adrian and myself with a T shirt each with the Logo on in recognition of the help with travel and tickets for Sky Blue International members.

Burton Albion
Ground – Pirelli Stadium

The ground holds just under 7,000 and on the one side has the attractive Main Stand. The other three sides were terraces on our visits. The Sky Blue Army were in the East Terrace with those seated in a section of the Main Stand.

It is a 25 minute walk from the town centre pubs and railway station.

Results
06 Sep 2015	2-1	League One	(Tudgay, Vincelot)
17 Nov 2018	0-1	League One	
14 Sep 2019	0-0	League One	

The early kick off for the Sunday game at Burton in September 2015, which was shown on Sky TV, meant leaving London just before 9am to arrive into Burton for 11.30. The day before the game the West Midlands Police were advising that pubs in central Burton would not be opening before midday, if at all that day.

Pub

We had already arranged to visit the **Old Cottage Tavern,** away from the town centre. Jane re-confirmed they were opening at 11.30 as usual and expecting us. We were certainly well looked after! The Old Cottage Tavern didn't provide food and when asked if they would allow us to bring in our own food (due to the very early start for some that day) Jane offered to provide sandwiches. Those who pre ordered were treated to ham and cheese rolls (batches for those from Coventry). Jane wouldn't take any money for them and suggested we might like to contribute to their Sunday raffle.

Barry, our ticket man, was quickly on the case. He circulated the pub and collected what was a record amount. The story is told he was suggesting to some of the locals in the pub it was for our new striker!

The raffle result was all square. Member Geoff Moore won one of the prizes with the other going to a Burton supporter.

By November 2018, the Old Cottage Tavern had closed its doors. Burton is well known for its brewing and excellent pubs. Following some research we contacted Carl and Nicki at the **Burton Bridge Inn**.

The 17th century pub is the flagship of the Burton Bridge estate and fronts the brewery itself. Food on match days was limited to cold cobs (batches), pork pies and bar snacks. They were prepared, given our numbers, to provide a curry for our group in the upstairs bowling alley area, which we were given exclusive use of. It was too noisy for some who found seats downstairs. The 24 members who opted for the curry were very impressed.

CCLSC members were popular that day with YouTube. We were joined at the Burton Bridge Inn, before the game by Adam Bostock, who produces *Sky Blue Social* on YouTube. The short video gave an insight into CCLSC's day out, and a link was provided in our next monthly newsletter. Carl and Nicki's 14 year old son, who ran a brewers VBlog channel on YouTube, asked several members questions on camera.

Also joining us that day was Rune Nyman, (pictured with Barry) a Norwegian who lives in Sweden. Rune had been to the Ricoh on several occasions to watch the Sky Blues but he was attending his first away game for several years.

By the time we next played at Burton, in September 2019, and remembering that we had been treated extremely well on our last visit to Burton, I again contacted Carl. He informed me he had recently purchased another pub in Burton but would be happy to provide food again, on a pre ordered basis. The Burton Bridge Inn still didn't do food at weekends. **The Devonshire Arms** was one of the better pubs we visited that season, with the beers, curry and welcome of the highest order. They served three Burton Bridge beers, Bass and guest ales.

A couple of members, including myself had booked hotel accommodation in Burton as the fixture was moved to a Friday evening, because the Derbyshire Police didn't want Derby v Cardiff and Coventry at Burton on the same day, However, Sky TV picked the Derby game for their Friday evening game. The Burton game was reverted to the Saturday. We watched Derby on TV that Friday evening in Burton.

The Devonshire Arms didn't have Sky TV but we did drop into the Derbyshire Arms on the Friday evening to say hello. Carl said he was somewhat concerned that he didn't have a separate room for us, like at the Burton Bridge Inn.

He served the curry at noon in a small snug area. Fortunately, the weather was very kind and the paved garden patio area was taken over by our members, easing any overcrowding concerns.

Members in the sunshine in the patio area are shown opposite.

Bury
Ground – Gigg Lane

Gigg Lane was a smallish and rather old fashioned ground despite the refurbishments in the 1990's. It was shared with FC United back in 2013. The Sky Blue Army were housed in the East Stand (pictured). The supporting pillars were a nuisance for those at the back of the stand when we had a large following.

Results

16 Feb 2013	2-0	League One	(Clarke, Baker)
24 Sep 2015	1-2	League One	(Johnson)
28 Feb 2017	1-2	League One	(Beavon)

Pub

The **Trackside Bar** situated in the waiting room on the platform of the East Lancashire Railway, was on many members "must visit" lists. Set against the backdrop of the East Lancashire Railway, the Trackside boasted an ever changing range of up to nine hand pulled cask ales, including their house beer, Piston Broke. Hot food and snacks were available.

It was often mentioned at the CCLSC AGM that if you only went to one North West game a season you should go to Bury for the Trackside Bar. For those who joined us at the Rat Race at Hartlepool, the Trackside is similar, with the station platform providing an outdoor seating area.

On our first visit in February 2013, the week after Mark Robins had left as Manager; members, who included a number from the North of England, were treated to a real steam train gala. Those savvy drinkers amongst us realised that we should get our beers in before the next scheduled train arrived as the Steam enthusiasts had their own beer break before continuing on their journey. We struck up a conversation with a fan who had a "banning" order from most football grounds, but who went out of his way to book taxis to get us to the ground. We also got into conversation with a grandfather, father and son who had been to the Ricoh earlier in the season. They travelled regularly following Bury away from home and as we chatted discovered we had frequented many of the same pubs around the lower league clubs.

In September 2015, on our next visit, it was also an especially long day for the Bury game. Due to the Rugby World Cup, and Man Utd unusually playing at home on a Saturday at 3pm, our group travel from London left Euston at 9 am and had to return via Warrington to get sensible ticket prices.

The Trackside bar that day had a Diesel Gala Event. It proved interesting to see football supporters and rail enthusiasts on the platform together watching these old diesel engines pulling into the station. We were joined that lunchtime at various intervals by the likes of "Ernest", "Eric" and "Capt Bill Smith" pulling into the station.

On a Tuesday evening in February 2017, despite the cold evening and depressing circumstances the team found itself in (we were to be relegated that season), we had several members at the Trackside. Pictured are Ben, Barry and Kev at the ground trying to be cheerful, despite the traffic problems that evening.

Everyone was therefore looking forward to the Bury away game, originally scheduled for September 2019 and a return to the Trackside. I had a holiday booked returning on the Friday so i could travel north to Bury the following day. It was to be a blank Saturday with no football to watch.

The game never took place of course following Bury's expulsion from the EFL.

Cambridge United
Ground – Abbey Stadium

The ground, with a capacity of just over 8,000 has two traditional stands running along the side of the pitch. The Sky Blue Army were in the modern South Stand, pictured, behind the goal. It was a good sized single tiered stand. The North Terrace at one end of the ground is covered. However, it only runs for about half the width of the pitch, with one side ending in line with the eighteen yard box. Thus there is a large open area at one corner of the ground that is unused for spectators but houses the supporters club.

Members will recall walking through Coldham Common, a muddy field, to get to the away turnstiles.

Results
04 Dec 2016   0-4   FA Cup
16 Sep 2017   1-2   League Two   (Nazon)

Pub

We met Cambridge in the FA Cup in December 2016. With the Sunday 2pm kick off at Cambridge, Kyle, the manager at the **Devonshire Arms,** a five minutes' walk from the station, recommended that we pre-booked our Sunday roasts. Those who did were very impressed that the food arrived on the dot at 12.30. The landlord also sold a further number of roasts, that hadn't been pre ordered, to our larger than expected group. With the performance being what it was, a 4-0 defeat, JB and Charles left early returning to the pub. They were informed that, much to the annoyance of regulars who had come in later for their Sunday Lunch, by the time our group left at around 1.30 there was no food left. This was probably a first, causing beer to run out has been achieved on several occasions, but I can't recall our group eating all the food!

Ben Sprung and his two boys pictured below.

We returned after our relegation the following season, in September 2017, to the Devonshire Arms, with its wooden booths and large tables, and again enjoyed their Milton Brewery beers. The amusing part of that day was the Cambridge mascot, Bob the Builder, being ejected from the ground by the police for winding up the Sky Blue Army.

Carlisle United
Ground – Brunton Park

Brunton Park, with a capacity of just below 18,000 has a number of unusual features. We were usually seated in the East Stand, pictured. The Main Stand opposite has a terraced paddock in front. There is an open terrace behind one of the goals with a small section of seating. The SBA were sold tickets here for the 2013 game but with the game moved to the Sunday, those attending were moved into the seating area in the East Stand.

Results

13 Jan 2013	0-1	League One	
17 Aug 2013	4-0	League One	(Clarke 2, Moussa, Daniels)
30 Dec 2017	1-0	League Two	(McNulty)

We were to travel to Carlisle twice in 2013. The January fixture was moved 24 hours, to a snowy Sunday, as our JPT match against Preston had been moved to Thursday evening for Sky. As our train was about 30 minutes out of Carlisle we got a very heavy snow storm. Charles and I were concerned that having travelled this far and with the extra expense the game wouldn't go ahead. The train fares back then were about £50 for a return from London and for the rearranged Sunday game we had paid a further £40 or so.

Pub

Many of the original travellers didn't travel the following day so there was only a handful of travelling members who met at the **Kings Head**, the CAMRA Branch Pub of the Year for 2012, located by the Lanes shopping centre.

We were back in September but Mike, the landlord, was not able to welcome us back as he was travelling that day, in the opposite direction, to see his team Arsenal play at the Emirates.

Smiling away are Chris Lambert, left, Bob Kane and Jo Harris. Not surprising with a 4-0 away day win.

A large number of members travelled to the match at Carlisle in December 2017. Our new policy for that season of using

Family Friendly pubs meant we needed to "find" a new pub before the Carlisle game. The King's Head operated a strictly over 18 policy, so after some research we were made welcome at the Grade ll listed **Howard's Arms,** serving Robinson's and Theakston beers. Member Phil Higgins raved so much about the pub, especially the food, and suggested we should have a Pub of the Season award.

The following season we introduced such an award.

The Landlord was happy to reserve tables for us in the back room, as long as we were happy to share it with the Carlisle London Supporters Club who always reserved a single table before each home game. When explaining our likely numbers, his only concern was whether the room would be large enough to accommodate all the CCLSC members.

Charlton Athletic
Ground – The Valley

When the Club extended the new two-tiered stand they enclosed the corners creating a stand holding 9,000. The overall capacity of the Valley is 27,000. The older South Stand, where the Sky Blue Army congregated looks somewhat out of place in an otherwise smart stadium. The ground has one solitary supporting column in the entire ground (pictured). It is right in the middle of the away supporters end.

Records
15 Oct 2016   0-3   League One
06 Oct 2018   2-1   League One   (Bakayoko 2)

Pub

We visited the **White Swan** in Charlton Village, in both October 2016 and October 2018. Both games will be remembered by Sky Blue supporters for different reasons, from the pigs to new songs. It is a 10-15 minute walk from Charlton station up a very steep hill.

For our second visit several members recalling the hill caught the local bus from outside Charlton station to the pub. The Swan has a large single room, with an L shaped bar and a large garden at the rear. It served 7 cask ales and has a large selection of bottled beers. The regular beers came from the Caveman brewery and the changing beers included Clarkshaws Phoenix Rising, Thornbridge Jaipur and Wadworth 6X. CAMRA members got 50p off a pint!

The 2016 game will be remembered more for the plastic pig protests, by both sets of supporters, than its football, a 0-3 defeat. Hundreds of plastic pigs were thrown onto the pitch as the game started delaying the game for several minutes.

Two seasons later on for our visit we had pre booked back at the White Swan. We were somewhat concerned when the Police were tweeting on the Friday evening that no pubs in the Charlton area were accepting Coventry fans the following day. They recommended pre match drinks should be in the London Bridge area. Interestingly, Aston Villa were playing Millwall that day and hundreds of their fans would be in the London Bridge area before the game, but the police co-ordinate such things don't they?

A panic phone call to the White Swan on Friday evening assured us they had not heard of any ban and that our group were expected. Sophie, the manager, even set aside over half the pub with tables reserved for us. Security on the door ensured that only Coventry fans and known locals were admitted.

The large Sky Blue Army at Charlton were in fine voice throughout the game that day and treated The Valley to a 10 minute plus rendition of *"Twist and Shout"* during a much better second half performance, before substitute Bakayoko scored the equaliser and then in the last minute headed the winner. The song 20 goals 20 goals was born. Don't you love a last minute winner?

Cheltenham Town
Ground – Whaddon Road (in 2018 named the Jonny-Rocks Stadium)

A small but smart ground with a capacity of 7,000. The Sky Blue Army was mainly in the Hazelwood Stand (pictured) with an additional 434 in the Colin Farmer Stand. Once again, the huge demand for tickets meant the away allocation of 1,345 was sold out the morning of going on sale.

Results
28 Apr 2018   6-1   League Two   (Bayliss, McNulty 3, Shipley, Biamou)

13 Nov 2018   0-2   FL Trophy

Pub

Our last away game of the 2017/18 season saw us at Cheltenham. **The Kemble Brewery**, a small back street pub where no brewing takes place these days, proved a great success. When we asked Caron the landlady whether she could welcome 30-40 of us wanting food she provided a one pot curry at midday for us. They usually provided "free" hot dogs on match days. Some had both the curry and hot dogs. As it was, over 70 turned up but Caron and her boys behind the bar did a fantastic job feeding us and keeping everyone in beer.

We left saying whilst we hoped we would not be playing Cheltenham the following season, but if we were, we would be back.

Pictured is SBI member Simon Fahy, from Canada, seen reminding everyone of the final score.

A couple of members did return in November 2018 for the FL Trophy game.

Chesterfield
Ground – Proact Stadium

The Proact Stadium is a modern stadium and holds 10,600. Both the stands running down the length of the pitch have curved roofs. Sky Blues supporters were in the North Stand behind one of the goals (pictured).

Pub

We were to first visit the **Derby Tup** in March 2015. The Tup was not in the CAMRA 2015 Good Beer Guide due to a change of owner at the time of selection, but came very highly recommended from the local Chesterfield CAMRA branch. The new licensee

Ade, from the nearby micro brewery Pigeon Fishers, had just taken over when we visited.

It is 1.8 miles from the station past the ground and is a 10 minute walk back to the ground. With its 10 handpumps, it featured beers from near and far, including Castle Rock Harvest Pale and Screech Owl along with Timothy Taylor's Landlord. The pub gets very full on match days, and Ade the manager, said he couldn't reserve an area for us. He was aware that those arriving by train, and either walking the 30 minutes or getting taxis from the station, would be outside just before the noon opening time. Our group did arrive just as it opened and we settled in a room at the back of the pub. We didn't realise the amount of Sky Blues fans that would use the Tup for their pre match drink, resulting in some members not being able to join us in the back room.

We were to return later that year on Monday 28 December 2015. Committee member Rob Parker completed his tour of the 92 Football League grounds when attending the game at Chesterfield that day. Rob, visiting family over the festive period, dropped into the Derby Tup a couple of days after our

visit. The Lady behind the bar said the Coventry City supporters visit on Christmas Monday had been their best ever trading day, with takings of £1,800.

The visit to the Derby Tup in January 2017 for the relegation six pointer saw our team lose, and for the second time that season a run of ten games without a win. Once again the Landlord opened up early and

allowed fish and chips to be consumed on the premises.
Arriving early ensured we were able to claim the back room.

Again for our final visit in September 2017 arriving at opening
time, we were able to claim our now customary back room
snug area.

Colchester United
Ground – JobServe Stadium

It is owned by the local council and was built at a cost of £14m and holds just over 10,000. It is quite bland in design, offering a very similar experience to the Ricoh in terms of all the facilities and view on offer. Unfortunately the whole ground is a soulless, concrete block that looks like it was made out of lego, built in the middle of nowhere. It is on the outskirts of Colchester, near the A12, sitting on a Business Park. In our visits the subsidised shuttle bus proved the best way to get out from the town to the stadium. The Sky Blue Army were in the North Stand in a stadium which especially in the concourse reminded many of the Ricoh.

Results

Date	Score	Competition	Scorers
20 Nov 2012	3-1	League One	(Moussa, Edjengyele, McGoldrick)
08 Mar 2014	1-2	League One	(Wilson)
22 Nov 2014	1-0	League One	(Madine)
14 Nov 2015	3-1	League One	(Murphy 2, Fortune)
13 Feb 2018	1-2	League Two	(Bayliss)
09 Nov 2019	2-0	FA Cup	(Shipley, McCallum)

Pictured opposite are the Davidson's Mark and Nikki (front), Lambo and Charles in the centre and Robin and George Ogleby (back) on the shuttle bus.

Pub

With our first visit an evening fixture, in November 2012, we met at the **Bricklayers Arms,** next to the station, taking the shuttle bus out to the stadium. The Adnams beers and a good range of guest beers made the Brick a good choice.

Pictured are Chris Lambert, Jim Mcillwaine, Bob Kane at the Brickmakers Arms.

In March 2014 we returned to the Bricklayers Arms. However, our policy of notifying the pub landlord of approximately how many members would be joining us for a pre match drink nearly came unstuck. The main group travelling from central London received a call from Charles as their train was pulling into Colchester. He was outside the pub and there was a large sign on the front door saying "Home fans only". I had spoken to the pub a few days earlier and had been given the ok that we would be welcomed. We were eventually allowed in the back door, settled down in the conservatory area and I discovered that it was the daughter of the landlord I had spoken with and she had forgotten to pass on the message. A visit by the local Police gave us the all clear saying "enjoy the game lads".

Interestingly, the majority of fans in the Bricklayers Arms that lunch time were Coventry supporters.

 The following season, we returned in November and met at the **Victoria Inn**, a few minutes' walk away from the station and in the wrong direction for the ground. The Bricklayers Arms had been criticised about beer selection and their home fans only rule so we investigated other pubs in the vicinity.

Andy the landlord at the Vic is a Blades fan and said he was looking forward to a group of away fans who were real ale drinkers. Whilst the Vic didn't do food, there were burger, pizza, fish and chips and curry houses all within 50 yards of the pub and we were welcome to bring food in to the pub.

On one occasion, Tim Fisher joined us before the game. The few Colchester fans in the Vic were very impressed and could not believe that the Chairman of a Football Club would visit and speak to supporters in a pub.

Sheena even notified us before our last visit in 2019, that the shuttle bus no longer ran but the few Colchester fans that were match day regulars would put us right. They did.

Both Andy and Sheena were away on holiday for our last visit, but arranged to open early, to coincide with our train from London. One of their guest beers for the day was Shortts 2 Tone Dark Mild. The barmaid said she hadn't seen this beer on tap before, so we speculated it was put on for our visit.

Crawley Town

Ground – Broadfield (renamed the People's Pension Stadium in December 2018)

Copyright Peter Bellamy

It has two small covered virtually identical terraces at each end, a squat main stand on one side, and on the other the East Stand which was opened in April 2012. This small ground has a capacity of 6,100. The Sky Blue Army were in the north stand terracing at one end of the ground (photo from Peter Bellamy).

Results

13 Apr 2013	0-2	League One	
03 Aug 2013	2-3	League One	(Wilson, Moussa)
03 May 2015	2-1	League One	(Tudgay, Maddison)
14 Apr 2018	2-1	League Two	(Ponticelli 2)

The April 2013 game was the first away league game against Crawley and for the August 2013 opening game of the season Crawley were only able to name five substitutes, instead of seven allowed.

Visits to Crawley will be remembered for the bad weather, crowd disturbances and the great escape.

Pub

For our first few visits we would meet at the **Swan**, a 10 minute walk from the station, which provided at the time the most extensive range of real ales in Crawley. There were two bars and an outside patio area. In April 2013 the awful conditions had calls for the game to be called off. We also heard the SBA sing "we want our money back" on several occasions during a miserable second half in the rain.

Four months later we were back for the opening day of the 2013/14 season. This time in the sunshine, many CCLSC members enjoyed pre match beers back at the Swan. Pictured above are members waiting for taxis. Robin Morden and Charles also pictured opposite inside the ground.

With the discussions on where we would play home games ongoing many fans were undecided whether or not they would go to "home" games. However, many sky blues fans on social media had stated that they will be going to away games. This put pressure on getting away day tickets for many of the games at the smaller grounds.

Tickets for the first game of the season away at Crawley in August certainly fell into that category. Crawley's ground capacity makes the Broadfield Stadium the smallest ground in League One. Indeed there are only 3 other grounds smaller in the whole of the football league. The away end holds 1,600, which was several hundred less than the Sky Blues fans were allocated for the opening game the previous season at Yeovil.

With the off field issues Crawley would not sell tickets via Coventry City and Charles had to pick up our tickets from the ground earlier in the day before returning to the Swan. The crowd disturbances during the match which were aimed at the owners put a dampener on the day.

For the next visit it was for the last game of the season on a Sunday in May 2015. It was a 12.15pm kick off. Travel was disrupted that day with a bus replacement service from Three Bridges to Crawley.

The Swan didn't open until noon on a Sunday and as the ground was only 2.2 miles from Three Bridges station members met at the **Snooty Fox,** opposite Three Bridges station AFTER the match. Not a Good Beer Guide pub and so not a pub we would normally visit but the kick off time and the bus replacement services dictated the venue. As it turned out muted celebration drinks were held. Twenty minutes from the end of the game we were being relegated, but two late goals meant we won and with other results going our way that Sunday the team finished well away from the relegation places.

The Swan had unfortunately closed by the time of our next visit in April 2018. We met at the **Brewery Shades** in the High Street. Arguably the oldest building in the High Street it served up to ten cask ales and provided CAMRA discounts. With the numbers attending pre ordering food was necessary.

Norwegians Lars (pictured on the far left) and Christian (far right) joined us at the Brewery Shades before the Crawley game. Also joining us was Helsinki based, Hannu (centre)

Crewe Alexandra
Ground – Alexandra Stadium (although widely referred to as Gresty Road)

The Sky Blue Army were always housed in the Whitby Morrison Stand (pictured) along one side of the pitch and opposite the large main stand, which dominates the ground and holds 7,000 out of the overall capacity of 10,000. The other three stands are roughly of the same height, covered and all seated, but are rather small in comparison.

Results

Date	Score	Competition	Scorers
01 Sep 2012	0-1	League One	
05 Feb 2013	2-0	Johnstones	(Clarke, Ellis og)
29 Mar 2014	2-1	League One	(Wilson 2)
11 Oct 2014	1-2	League One	(Grant (og))
02 Jan 2016	5-0	League One	(Armstrong 3 Murphy 2)
17 Mar 2018	2-1	League Two	(Ray (og), Bayliss)

Pub

In September 2012, we met at **Hops**, about a mile from the ground. It was the CAMRA Cheshire Pub of the Year in 2011 and well worth finding with its four guest beers and a comprehensive range of Belgian draught and bottled beers available. For the JPT Area Final second leg in February 2013 we went for a different pub for the mid week game rather than returning to the pub we had enjoyed earlier in the season.

The Hops had worked well, with its large beer range and outside terrace in the September sunshine, but is was felt to be just too far from the ground and perhaps not large enough for an evening game. For the JPT game we went to a pub slightly nearer the ground, the **Borough Arms**. It was 0.9 mile from the station but away from the High Street pubs which were crowded, rarely served real ale and not in the best of condition. The Borough Arms was full of city fans before the away leg. Similar to the Spurs game earlier in the year, CCLSC members contributed to the selling out of several beers that night as the talk was of great comebacks and lots of hope. The 2-0 win was probably the worst result we could have had (we had lost the first leg 3-0), as deep into injury time the McSheffrey free kick gave us hope of an equaliser, and extra time. Many had left the ground to dash the 5 minutes to the station, to get the last train back to London, missing the final moments. Those that stayed overnight, like Charles and i, toured the High Street pubs to be constantly informed there was no beer left as "you lot had drank it all". We did find a pub, with real ale, having walked nearly back to the Borough Arms, to drown our sorrows.

The Borough Arms, the home of the Borough Arms brewery, has up to nine handpumps serving a wide range of ales, mainly from small and micro breweries. Members were tempted with the brewery's own Blonde Temptation (it is a beer I can confirm) and Borough Gold.

It then became our regular for the league visits in March and October 2014. At the Crewe game in March we were joined by Andy Ward, from Scotland, who insisted on paying for his match ticket in Scottish currency, to the great amusement of Barry and fellow members. The old jokes about it being legal tender abounded.

We were joined at the October game by our Swiss friends, Marcus and his son Joel, with Andrea and Albi Mozer. Marcus and Joel had been over to the Arsenal game earlier this year and for Joel he was to see a big difference between a full Emirates and Gresty Road. Regular SBI visitors Albi and Andrea flew into Manchester from Zurich and joined us at the Borough Arms.

January 2016 saw us return once again to the Borough Arms. Armstrong scored a hat-trick and Murphy scoring two in a 5-0 win.

For the March 2018 game, returning to the Borough Arms, which still remains one of our favourite away pubs, Mike the Landlord was apologetic when we arrived saying that a number of his locals were in the area we normally reserve, as they wanted to watch the Six Nations Rugby on the TV. He opened the downstairs bar especially for us. Many regulars at the Borough Arms over the years hadn't realised it had a downstairs bar!

Watching the Sky Blues, especially after a long distance journey is not always in the sunshine as weather at the 2018 game showed! Ross and George showing it is grim up north.

Dagenham & Redbridge
Ground – Victoria Road (Chigwell Construction Stadium)

A small tidy ground with a capacity of 6,000 had open terracing behind one goal and covered terracing along the side of the pitch. We were certainly introduced to life in the lower leagues with four balls being kicked out of the ground on our visit. The Sky Blue Army were housed in the modern West Stand behind the goal (pictured).

Result
14 Aug 2012   1-0   League Cup   (Kilbane)

Pub

No CCLSC travel was planned for the Dagenham away Capital One Cup match in August 2012, but several members met in the **Eastbrook** in Dagenham Road prior to the match. It is one of Britain's Real Heritage Pubs and was popular with Sports fans in an area that had little real ale. Following this game, the pub and directions emails became the norm to alert CCLSC members where we were meeting for pre match drinks.

We were certainly introduced to "life" in the lower leagues. Simon Fahy who arrived late, commented that he wasn't sure that a match was on, with the lack of people around, as he walked from the station, past the ground, to meet other CCLSC members at the Eastbrook.

Doncaster Rovers
Ground –Keepmoat Stadium

Keepmoat Stadium was opened in 2007 and was built by, and owned by, Doncaster Council. It is a medium-sized modern all seated ground, rather bland but comfortable. It has a capacity of 15,000. The ground it well away from anywhere, set in a park next to a lake near the racecourse and the old Bell Vue ground.. The Football Ground Guide believes it is the only league ground to be next to a lake. Sky Blues fans were in the North Stand, pictured, in surroundings that feel like a smaller version of the Ricoh, only in red.

Results

15 Dec 2012	4-1	League One	(McGoldrick 2, Moussa, Barton)
26 Dec 2014	0-2	League One	
23 Apr 2016	0-2	League One	
04 May 2019	0-2	League One	
18 Jan 2020	1-0	League One	(Shipley)

The December 2014 game saw Adam Barton and James Maddison both receive a second yellow card and were both sent off in a mad two minute spell in the 74th and 76th minute.

Pub

As the stadium is on the outskirts of town, and there is not much choice in the way of pubs near the ground, we met on several occasions at the **Corner Pin,** which is conveniently situated for the town centre and railway station. For our visits in December 2012, Boxing Day 2014, April 2016 and May 2019 the Corner Pin proved an excellent choice. It was the local CAMRA Pub of the Year 2011, 2014 and 2015 serving beers from local breweries and offered CAMRA discount to members.

Members will probably also recall the giant Yorkshire roasts, as much as the excellent beers, that Ruth and Dave served.

We made our final visit to the Corner Pin for the last game of the season in May 2019. With the 17.30 kick off, we reserved tables at 2pm and as Ruth said, "you kept us busy". The large support had of course purchased tickets in anticipation of a promotion push. Doncaster went to the playoffs, rather than us, that day.

Ruth and Dave were to leave the Corner Pin the week after our visit in May 2019 and we joined them at their new pub, **The (Little) Plough** in January 2020. The two roomed bar close to the station, served Acorn Barnsley Bitter and Bradfield Farmers Blonde as regular beers. The interior dates back to 1934 and is mentioned in the CAMRA National Inventory of Historical Pub Interiors. The Little Plough didn't do food, so no giant Yorkshires this time, but Ruth and Dave did provide large bowls of chips with bread buns (a batch to those from Coventry) in the lounge area they reserved for us.

Exeter City
Ground – St James' Park

Exeter were undergoing major re-development of their ground at the time of our only visit and the EFL had granted them special permission for a significantly reduced away allocation of just 350. The Sky Blues Army were located in one side of the Main Stand (pictured). The stand opposite had been demolished at the time and the usual away terrace behind the goal was closed to allow for the heavy machinery to get into the ground.

Results
13 Jan 2018   0-1   League Two

Our one trip to Exeter in January 2018 will be remembered for the scramble to get match tickets, due to Exeter's ground improvements closing their away end. The SBA had only 350 supporters at Exeter (if you count only those in the away end). We were fortunate that many of our regular travellers were able to get their hands on tickets or tickets in the home end.

Pub

The **Mill on the Exe** before the game was very spacious with our group having the large area in the conservatory room reserved for us. They served St Austell beers. It was a paper mill until 1960 and the original water wheel used to turn the machinery is now a feature in the garden.

The staff greeted us with "you are the football supporters, yes, we have reserved an area for you". Our policy of locating pubs away from the ground (in this case 1.5 miles from the ground) clearly worked, as the Mill was not on the usual football supporters list of pubs.

Fleetwood Town
Ground – Highbury Stadium

A typical quiz question these days is who plays at Highbury? Older members may have been to the other Highbury in our Premier League days!

Fleetwood's Highbury holds just over 5,000 and is a modern stadium with good facilities and views. The Main stand running alongside the stadium is a very aesthetically pleasing stand and is all seated. Opposite this stand is the Highbury stand and this stretches just half the length of the pitch. At either end are the Percy Ronson Stand and the Memorial Stand. Both are covered terraces. Each stand offers a good view. The Sky Blue Army were predominantly in the Percy Ransom terrace at one end of the ground. Those with seating were in the Parkside Stand.

Results
17 Mar 2015   2-0   League One   (Samuel, Nouble)
10 Oct 2015   1-0   League One   (Wood (og))
03 Sep 2016   0-2   League One
27 Nov 2018   0-3   League One
28 Jan 2020   0-0   League One

Our experiences have shown that taking the tram from Blackpool is one of the most scenic and pleasant ways to travel to a match. It does however take 45 minutes from Blackpool!

Pub

We took the tram ride out to Fleetwood, for pre match drinks and food at the **Strawberry Gardens**, a free house that served over 12 real ales. Syd Little (part of the comedians Little & Large) with his wife Sheree ran the "Little Restaurant" at the Strawberry Gardens.

Several of our trips to Fleetwood have been midweek evening games. This has reduced the number of members joining us.

For the midweek March 2015 game, on St Patrick's Day, a small number of members made the journey staying overnight in Blackpool.

The group initially met at the **Bispham Hotel** in Blackpool, pictured, a Sam Smith Brewery pub. We said we might come back when playing Blackpool later in the season but realised that is was just too far out of the centre and in the wrong direction away from the ground.

The evening ended at the Irish Bar on Blackpool front which, despite allowing us to buy further drinks suddenly announced they were closing early – on St Patricks' Day!

We were back six months later in October 2015, this time on a Saturday. We returned to the Strawberry Gardens and again were served a rather slow lunch by the entertaining Syd Little in his restaurant.

He wanted to "perform" and pose for photos at each table. As Syd was serving the food, one of the group said they had ordered mushy peas. Syd, ever the comedian, told him to smash them with his spoon. He did bring out a bowl with mushy peas a couple of minutes later.

By September 2016 Syd Little had moved from the Strawberry Gardens. That day will be remembered for the 600 mile round trip, the poor team performance on the day, pouring rain, and the Virgin train return into Euston being heavily delayed. It really stretched everyone's commitment. Following the 2-0 defeat we were 23rd in the League.

The pub was very full with Sky Blues supporters that day, but fortunately our group of 20 plus had a private area put aside by Annie.

Thanks to the EFL we were back for another midweek game in November 2018. There was a small group of us, pictured, who met at the **Pump & Truncheon** in central Blackpool before the tram ride out to Fleetwood. We received some sad news that day that the Pump was closing down the following month.

Upon arrival into Fleetwood we enjoyed a meal at the Strawberry Gardens before the game. Unfortunately, they ran out of real ale, so after the game refreshments were at two Wetherspoon pubs in Blackpool.

In January 2020, another midweek game saw the group of members, pictured, meeting at the **Layton Rakes,** a Wetherspoon pub, in central Blackpool for food as the reports from the local CAMRA branch indicated that the Strawberry Gardens were still not serving real ale midweek in the winter months. Upon reaching Fleetwood we had a final pre match drink at the **Royal Oak.** The beer choice, not necessarily the quality of the beers and the local name "Dead Uns" probably summed up the place. As a result it was the tram back into Blackpool for late night drinks

Forest Green Rovers
Ground – The New Lawn

The New Lawn is in the picturesque village of Nailsworth. It is on the top of a very steep hill. The Stadium which has a capacity of just over 5,000 is dominated by the Main Stand on one side of the pitch. The Sky Blue Army were in the West Terrace on the opposite side of the ground, shown on the left in the photo. This terrace has a capacity of around 1,000 and runs the full length of the pitch. The uncovered terrace made it difficult to really make some noise which dampened down the atmosphere somewhat. Apart from disabled fans, Forest Green only provided seating for 10 visiting supporters, CCLSC had three of these. The entrance to the away terrace was at the back of the stadium from the main entrance. It has relatively poor access, so there were long queues as we had sold out our allocation.

Results
03 Feb 2018   **1-2**   **League Two**   **(McNulty)**
08 Oct 2019   **0-0**   **FL Trophy**

Pub

We only played one League game, at the New Lawn, in February 2018. This will be remembered for the poor team performance and pouring rain whilst standing on open terracing. Luckily the pub saved the day! The lack of a station

or CAMRA GBG real ale pubs in Nailsworth, combined with not everyone wanting to try the vegan beer at the ground, we met at the **Ale House**, in Stroud. It is a 3 minute walk from the station. The Grade II listed building opposite the Cornhill Farmers Market served Cotswold Lion Golden Fleece, Dark Star Hophead, and Stroud Budding, with up to six other changing beers. It was the Local Branch CAMRA Pub of the Year and family friendly. Nigel the landlord looked after us allocating a side room and the adjacent area for our group.

Taxis from Stroud worked well. We were advised that getting away from the ground after the game, and back to Stroud for our train, could be problematical. The larger than expected attendance (the SBA had sold out its allocation) would grid lock the one road down the hill from the ground. Taxis were booked for fulltime and we were to be picked up halfway down the hill. Everyone arrived at the taxis on time. The rain and performance helped. We were all back into Stroud a few minutes later, enjoying an unexpected further pint at the Ale House before our onward journey home.

The evening FL Trophy game in October 2019 saw a couple of members drinking at the ground. Forest Green Rovers were to win the penalty shoot out 8-7 and were awarded a bonus point.

Gillingham
Ground – Priestfield Stadium

Priestfield has a capacity of 11,500 and has an impressive two tiered main stand and the Rainham End, for home fans, provides an impressive backdrop. Walking up Priestfield Road towards the away end the view in front of you at all our visits resembled a construction site with the amount of scaffolding on show. The Sky Blues Army were in the uncovered Brian Moore stand named in memory of the legendary commentator and lifelong Gills fan, Brian Moore (pictured).

Results
11 Mar 2014	2-4	League One	(Wilson, Baker)
17 Jan 2015	1-3	League One	(Madine)
02 Apr 2016	0-0	League One	
24 Sep 2016	1-2	League One	(Reid)
25 Aug 2018	1-1	League One	(Clarke-Harris)

The March 2014 game was unique. We lost 4-2 but there were four penalties scored that day, two for each side.

Pub

The **Will Adams**, a small single-bar, named after the local navigator and adventurer, has been our go to pub when playing the Gills. It has been the Branch CAMRA Pub of the Year twice in recent years. It always had three or four real ales on sale plus draught cider. There is a special football food menu of pie, chips and beans etc when Gills are at home and the Landlord, Pete, a Gills fans welcomes real ale drinking away fans (even the odd lager drinker he says). He has opened early for us for evening and Saturday games over the years.

Ross and Ross are pictured with the group packed into the bar.

We had return visits in March 2014, January 2015, April 2016, September 2016 and in August 2018. Our planned visit in 2020 did not materialise due to the curtailment of the season.

Everyone who attended games at Priestfield will remember two things.

One, the Sky Blue Army were in the open in the temporary seated stand situated on top of an existing terrace. When I say temporary, the scaffolding has been there since our visit in the Championship in 2003-4 when we won 5-2. That game will always be remembered for the goal scored very late in the game by Richard Shaw. This was his only goal for the club.

Gillingham FC did issue plastic raincoats when it rained. Several members missed the goal straight after half time in August 2018 whilst collecting their cagoules in torrential rain.

Second, it will be remembered by those trying to find the Will Adams. Whilst it is only 0.4 mile from the station you had to walk down a very small footpath, opposite the station entrance, into a park. Whilst in the park you then had to find the path over the railway bridge which emerged into a housing estate. Missing the small park entrance meant a longer detour down the High Street.

Grimsby Town
Ground – Blundell Park

Blundell Park has a capacity of 9,000 and has covered ends behind both goals with the two-tier Findus stand on side opposite the Main Stand. Away fans are usually in one corner of the Osmond Stand (pictured) where just fewer than 600 supporters can be accommodated. However for the large Sky Blue Army 1,800 tickets were obtained and we were given the complete stand.

The ground is about a mile from Cleethorpes, not Grimsby, station and takes about 20 minutes to walk.

Results
12 Aug 2017   2-0   League Two   (McNulty, Grimmer)

The opening game of the 2017/18 season was our only visit. I was desperate to go as I hadn't been to Grimsby before; it would be another new ground for me, even if it wasn't in Grimsby, but Cleethorpes. My daughter was about to give birth with her first baby, and our first grandchild. We had spoken the evening before and she had no indication that anything would happen over the weekend. You should go she said.

Pub

So I set off with a large group on the journey in August 2017 arriving into Cleethorpes prior to noon. Members were impressed with the clean and tidy sea front as we took the 10 minute walk along the front to **Willy's**. The pub brewed Willy's Original on the premises and the brewery could be seen from the bar.

The pub also served Bass and two other guest ales and had spectacular views over the River Humber and the beach. The landlady had suggested she open the upstairs room for us, given our large numbers. We therefore had our own private room at Willy's. Being upstairs, we had a good view of not only the sea and beach but the police presence at the pub further up the road. We could see several police vans, some from as far away as County Durham, in attendance to what was deemed a high profile game. Again our policy of pre booking with pub landlords, away from the ground, paid dividends.

I of course, had a call at 1.30pm, in Willy's, to say I had become a grandpa. It wasn't quite the biggest cheer of the day when I returned to the upstairs room, but it wasn't far off.

We had time for an after match drink and were celebrating our win (and the birth of my grandson, Sam, that day). We enjoyed these at the No 1 Pub, at the station, with its Batemans and Bass beers. This small pub proclaims to be a train pub not a chain pub, according to the sign. Well worth a visit but unfortunately, much too small for our pre match drinks.

Hartlepool United
Ground – Victoria Park

Victoria Park was a typical lower league ground with a capacity of less than 8,000. The Sky Blue Army were packed into a small covered end stand (pictured), with a tea hut to one side – no alcohol was served. There were a couple of pillars to block our view.

We discovered on our first trip that Hartlepool fans prefer to be called *The Monkey Hangers?* It is said that the residents of Hartlepool famously hanged a monkey that had washed up from a ship sunk during the Napoleonic wars, because they thought the monkey was a French spy!

Results

17 Nov 2012	5-0	League One	(Baker 2, Barton, McGoldrick, Moussa)
07 Dec 2013	1-1	FA Cup	(Baker)

Pub

The Rat Race Ale House, couldn't be handier for the railway station, there being an entrance to it from the station platform! It's less than 10 minutes walk from the ground and was wonderfully informal, though very small. It does not have a bar (!), with available beers chalked up on the wall, with samples of the beers available shown in test tubes, and served direct from the cask from an adjoining room. They are served to you at your table. It served an ever-changing range of real ales and real cider. It did not serve lager, fizzy beer or cider and does not serve food.

Opening at 12.02 (said historically to coincide with train arrivals), those taking advantage of cheaper group travel arrived into Hartlepool in November 2012 at 11 am, and went to the **Ward Jackson**, a Wetherspoon pub, for food before returning to the Rat Race when it opened.

Charles reminds me that I had spare 50p CAMRA beer vouchers that were due to expire in December. So as we entered the Ward Jackson, I shared them out and Charles, first at the bar and buying his first pint of the day, was informed that he could not use his voucher.

When trying to explain they were still valid the barmaid calmly stated that the discount could not be applied on beers valued under £1. Charles had ordered the house beer, at £1.49 a pint, resulting in the discounted price falling below the £1 minimum. The group of us were willing to accept a 49p discount we said, which had the bar staff struggling, as no one else had done that before!

We were to return in December 2013 in the FA Cup. A small band of CCLSC members made the long journey north for the FA Cup game against Hartlepool.

Early train arrival meant that we were to repeat the early lunch at the Ward Jackson before our pre match drinks at the Rat Race.

It was back to one of last season's favourite pubs. The Rat Race is probably one of the smallest pubs we have ever been and has double yellow lines on some of the tables so the landlord can get to the tables to serve the beer. If you want to use the toilet, following the signs, you end up on the station platform to use the station facilities.

Ipswich Town
Ground – Portman Road

The ground, with a capacity of 30,000, had improved since our Championship visits following the re-development of both stands behind the goals. As a result the two stands on the side of the pitch look tired in comparison. The Sky Blues Army were in one side of the Cobbold Stand along the side of the pitch (pictured).

Results
10 Dec 2019   2-1   FA Cup   (Shipley, Biamou)
07 Mar 2020   1-0   League One   (Godden)

We were to play away at Ipswich twice within a few months of each other. In December 2019 in the FA Cup replay, and what was our final fixture in March 2020, before the season was curtailed.

One curious fact was that we played Ipswich three times in the space of ten days in December 2019. A Birmingham "home" league game and the FA Cup 2nd Round both ended in draws before we won the replay at Portman Road. The Sky Blues were to win the more important league game in March 2020. We did not know it at the time but this was to be the final game of the season.

For the FA Cup replay members met at the **Station Hotel**, which as the name suggests is opposite the main station. It is the designated away fans pub with heavy security and serves the Greene King beers in plastic glasses.

For the league game, we ventured some 15 minute walk away from the station and in the opposite direction to the ground, for our designated pub, the **Steamboat Tavern**. Travel that day was disrupted with planned bus replacement services between Liverpool Street and Ingatestone. Members travelling were split up and arrived into Ipswich at different times. The

early arrivals, having passed the heavy security, had their first drinks in the Station Hotel. Those that did were pleased we had an alternative pub that day. The away fans pub was getting extremely crowded well before noon and there were stories of long delays in getting served as it approached kick off time.

The Steamboat Tavern, with its riverside views, was a great find serving four guest ales and hearty food. Andy, the landlord and the Steamboat crew were kept busy with a larger than expected group.

Murphy, the pub dog, was initially parading around with an Ipswich Town scarf round his neck. That was soon replaced by a Sky Blue one which he proudly wore around the pub that day.

The Steamboat was a 15 minute walk to the ground. By crossing the bridge by the marina rather than returning to the station it did cut down the journey time.

With the bus replacement service back to Ingatestone after the game it was a two hour journey back into central London.

CCLSC members later voted the Steamboat Tavern as their Pub of the Season 2019/20. With the pandemic restrictions we had to post the certificate to Andy.

I also notified the local CAMRA branch of the award and their reply was a classic. "Nice one. Thanks to all who voted. Good luck for next season in the Championship. Make sure you beat Norwich! (Some superb pubs there, mind!)"

Who would have thought there was football rivalry within CAMRA?

Leyton Orient
Ground – Brisbane Road (now the Breyer Group Stadium)

It is still known by many as Brisbane Road. Three sides of the ground were built in recent years, making the ground look quite smart. Guess where the Sky Blue Army were? Yes, in the tatty old East Stand with uncomfortable wooden seats, a low roof and a couple of pillars to obscure our view. The corners of the ground are filled with residential flats. This proved entertaining for the SBA when one resident came onto their balcony during the game. "You are only here to see the City" was the chant.

Results

27 Oct 2012	1-0	League One	(McGoldrick)
06 Aug 2013	2-3	League Cup	(Baker, Moussa)
08 Oct 2013	0-0	Johnstones Paint	
28 Jan 2014	0-2	League One	
01 Nov 2014	2-2	League One	(O'Brien 2)

I am not certain whether it was the draw of a brewery tour or not, but Orient prompted the season's biggest pub support for our first visit.

Pub

In October 2012 we met at the **King William IV,** in the High Street. It was a traditional East London pub and the home of Brodies Brewery. It offered a choice of 12-15 beers, mostly home brews.

Before the Orient match, 30 members, out of the much larger contingent, enjoyed a tour of the Brodies Brewery at the King William IV. Everyone was surprised how small and limited the facilities were given the large range of beers on offer. Barry Chattaway commented that if he added an extra metre to his garage he could start up a brewery!

Per Lauritson, a long standing SBI member from Denmark joined other CCSLC members with a number of his London based friends at the Brentford and Orient games. They proudly displayed, for the first time, his Danish Sky Blues on Tour flag outside the King William IV.

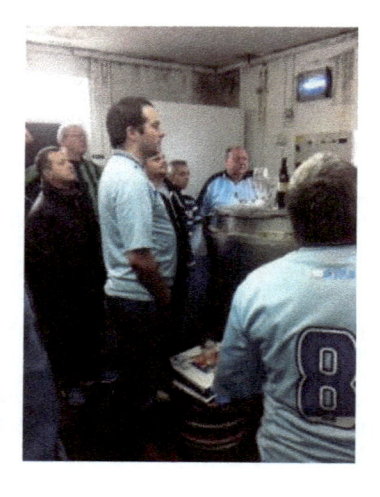

Despite informing the Landlord to expect a large number of CCLSC members at the King William IV, there were unfortunately long delays for drinks and food as a result of the limited number of staff on duty.

 As a result the **Birkbeck Tavern** was our designated pub for the three midweek evening kick offs in the Capital One Cup, Johnstone Paint Trophy and the League fixture in August 2013, October 2013 and January 2014. It is 0.3 miles from Leyton tube and Les, the Landlord, provided 6 real ales, including his house special Rita's. Despite being crowded we were well looked after, if suffering from slow service, on the first two visits.

Having called ahead for our third visit of the season to the Birkbeck, it was clear from the Landlady's attitude that she hadn't been informed. She was often the only one behind the bar, which at times was several deep waiting to be served. Les, the Landlord, was nowhere to be seen as the crowds increased.

For our visit in November 2014 we found a new pub for CCLSC to replace the Birkbeck, where slow service and the lack of bar staff was heavily criticised on our past visits. Lambo and Jim Mcilwaine did venture to the Birkbeck that day. They reported that Les had extra staff on and wondered where everyone was!

 CCLSC members met at the **Leyton Technical**, in High Road, Leyton in November 2014. It was in the old Leyton Town Hall, an 1896 building that later became the technical college. They served up to 8 varying cask ales including Thornbridge Jaipur.

The Leyton Technical, a short 5 minute walk from the ground, proved to be a hit. Sean, the manager, set aside a designated room for us, which was good thinking given the large number of members who turned up. Per and Jesper again proudly showed their "Danish Sky Blues on Tour" flag at the pub. They were politely asked to take the flag off the wall given the *Tech* was usually a "home" pub. Locals arriving after 1pm, for their pre match pint, were flabbergasted that their room and pub had away fans, and lots of them. The traffic was stopped on the Leyton High Road as our group left for the game, for that group photo.

Lincoln City
Ground – Sincil Bank Stadium

The 10,000 capacity Sincil Bank Stadium had a small odd looking stand opposite the Sky Blues Army located in the Stacey West Stand (pictured). It only runs half the length of the pitch straddling the half way line, with gaps at either end. One of these has been filled in with what is the Family stand. The Lincoln home support was the loudest singing choir we encountered that season. They gave a SBA a run for its money that day.

Results
18 Nov 2017   2-1   League Two   (Jones, Nazon)

Pub

We visited the **Jolly Brewer** on our only visit to Lincoln in November 2017. Many travelling to Lincoln that day had to stand, in what was a two carriage train, on the final part of the journey from Nottingham. We were met at Lincoln station by Committee member Rob

Parker, who had recently moved to Lincoln, and he bought a large box of biscuits to keep us going until the Jolly Brewer opened and lunch was served. On the way to the Jolly Brewer Rob took us via the Witch and Wardrobe, which opened before noon.

The Jolly Brewer, situated near the foot of Lindum Hill, was decorated in an Art Deco style, with a side room furnished with reclaimed cinema seats. It served three regular beers, Little Black Abbott, Tom Wood's Lincoln Gold, and Welbeck Henrietta, along with guest ales that were not often found locally. Good value food was also on offer. Mark, the landlord, went to the game himself and advised those wanting taxis to pre book them early from nearby Unity Square. The pub was about 1 mile from the ground.

Martin Scragg "Scraggy", who in the mid 1990's was the CCLSC Travel Secretary, also joined up at the Jolly Brewer. He had moved to Lincoln several years ago. It was good to catch up with him.

The Sky Blues played in grey and two late goals secured victory with Jodi Jones cutting in from the right to score one.

Luton Town
Ground – Kenilworth Road

Luton have wanted to move to a new ground for many years and therefore there has been limited re-development at Kenilworth Road, which holds 10,000. The Sky Blue Army were on one side of the Oak Road Stand (on the Executive Stand side and furthest away in the photo above) at one end of the ground. The entrance to the Oak Stand must be one of the most unusual in the country. After going down a rather small alleyway at the side of the stadium (or down the usually cordoned off Oak Road), the impression is of queuing to go into someone's house and then through their back garden to get into the stand! (pictured below).

Pub

We hadn't played at Luton for several years, and for the pre season visit back in 2015, we had an enjoyable pre match drink at the **English Rose.**

I hadn't contacted the pub beforehand as it was only a pre season friendly and we didn't think many members would travel. We were surprised that around 25 members turned up sitting in the garden/patio area on a sunny July day. The beers were of good quality. The landlord was pleasantly surprised by the number of football supporters, as he didn't get a large crowd on Saturday lunchtime from the mainly Asian local community. The pub is said to have been the haunt of Diana Dors who wed the landlord's son back in the 1950's. Upon later investigation and thinking we might return, we discovered the Rose closed in early 2017.

The previous season's Forecasting competition winner, Robin Morden caught up with Pat Raybould at Luton (pictured) to donate his prize money to the Junior Sky Blue's. Pat leads a team of volunteers who run activities in the Family Zone before every

weekend home game. The money was used to sponsor the JSB's subbuteo table, thus giving a more permanent presence rather than the money just going into the pot. Many members thought this was a wonderful gesture from Robin.

For our visit in October 2017, remembered for the Shipley free kick in the 3-0 win, many of the Luton town centre pubs were classified as "Home fans only", so consideration was given to a Barnet style central London pre match drink. The local CAMRA branch did suggest the **Black Horse**, a back street pub, outside the city centre, but in totally the wrong direction to the ground. It served 4 real ales, typically sourced from local breweries, Tring, Leighton Buzzard and Oakham. Traditional pub food was available.

Unfortunately, on first look this didn't seem to meet our needs, as it didn't open until 2pm on Saturday lunchtime. Speaking to the Landlord, and explaining the likely numbers of members attending, he agreed to open at noon to accommodate us. Given the police restrictions we encouraged all our members to be at the pub by noon. Those waiting outside at noon were greeted as the doors opened by Chris, the Landlord, frantically holding back a large growling dog. We thought we may have to show our CCLSC membership to get in! You know you are in the pub early when the landlord is seen munching his cornflakes behind the bar. It proved to be a little gem of a pub.

The barmaid had joined the queue waiting to get in at noon. This antipodean was magnificent, often serving three people at once, asking what one wanted, and pouring beers for another whilst taking the money from a third. The landlord's wife came round just after we all arrived, asking who wanted food. The menu consisted of pie, chips and a choice of beans or peas. It was £5 per meal.

John Bryant (JB) asked the landlord if they sold wine as he could not see any on display. They had some in the cellar and the landlord brought up a couple of bottles covered in dust. JB having chosen one asked how much for the glass or for the bottle? JB had a decent bottle of Merlot for £6. Maybe the normal clientele didn't drink wine. Rob Parker, a designated driver that day insisted on a photo!

At around 2.15 pm I was at the bar and overheard a local asking Chris, the landlord, who these people were. "You never usually have anyone in on a Saturday afternoon". Chris replied, "I had some guy call saying they wanted food and drinks from noon. They have eaten and drank me out of house and home".

For our next visit, in February 2019, with the noon kick off there was no time for pre match drinks. Pubs in central Luton were closed until after kick off. Our unbeaten February was overshadowed by the (then) EFL deadline being announced there was the possibility at their April meeting of expelling us from the League. There were demonstrations in front of the Sky TV camera as the long term future of our Club was in the balance. Unreserved seating meant many of our members were dispersed throughout the away end. Some did manage a quick pint near St Pancras before travelling out to Luton.

The police clearly did consider this a high risk match. Coaches were waiting outside the away end after the game to ferry supporters back to the station. Supporters were not allowed to walk through town back to the station. It was standing room only on our coach and the route back to the station avoided the town centre. The coach took so much time we were in danger of missing our pre booked train. The police were giving assurances that we would be at the station in time for the train. They seemed genuinely shocked when our group of six, on that particular coach, said that we were booked on the London train and not one going north. When we finally reached the station we had to run across the walkway and just caught our train.

Mansfield Town
Ground – One Call Stadium

The Stadium only uses three sides. The cantilevered stand along the side of the pitch holds over 5,500 with both stands behind the goals accommodating approximately 2,000 each. The Sky Blue Army were in the North Stand, which is unpopular with a number of home fans, as the North End of the ground had been the traditional home end for many years.

Results
24 Feb 2018   1-1   League Two   (Clarke-Harris)

Pub

We were to only visit Mansfield during our one season in League Two, in February 2018. We were made especially welcome at the **Railway Inn,** a 5 minute walk from the station. It had a main bar and two smaller rooms which Jane, the landlady, allocated for those on group travel who had pre-ordered food. It served four beers and a real cider.

Jane was concerned that the pub got very busy from around 1pm, with home fans on match days. Given this, we did manage to get food orders from the group, despite the extensive menu offered. We arrived into Mansfield at 11.27 and we were all seated, with drinks, by noon. Jane and the girls had serving lunch down to military precision and our pre ordered meals were served well before the pub got busy. Barry thanking the girls got a kiss for his trouble. I was a little miffed after all the organising I had done, but was rewarded with my own kiss on leaving for the game, much to the amusement of the members.

The Railway Inn also won appreciation for the sign of the year. "Dear Alcohol, we had a deal where you would make me funnier, smarter and a better dancer.... I saw the video, we need to talk!"

This was the game that we finally started to believe that promotion might be on. Mansfield were in the play off positions. Jordan Willis was sent off after 15 minutes but a battling performance and a late Jonson Clarke-Harris penalty saw a 1-1 draw. Mansfield manager Steve Evans resigned three day after the game.

One other memory of that day was that we had to run the gauntlet of a group of 14 year olds looking for trouble in the underpass from the station.

Millwall
Ground – The Den

Millwall moved the short distance from the original Den to what is known locally as the New Den in 1993. It is made up of four separate two-tiered stands with a capacity of 20,000. The Sky Blue Army were at one end of the ground in the North Stand upper tier (pictured).

Results

15 Aug 2015	4-0	League One	(Armstrong 2, Lameiras, O'Brien)
10 Sep 2016	1-1	League One	(Sordell)

Pub

There was some concern amongst members about advertising where we would be meeting for our pre match drinks in August 2015. We did say in our pub email that we would be meeting in the London Bridge area from around noon and plan to catch the 14.25 train from London Bridge for the 4 minute train ride to South Bermondsey. There is a covered walkway from the station platform directly to the away turnstiles.

Regular travellers and members were asked to contact committee members personally to be informed where we were meeting.

We apologised for the secrecy that shrouded the pub we were using in the London Bridge area before the game. The London Bridge and Borough Market areas get very crowded with tourists on Saturday lunchtime and as there was an England Rugby game on later that day, it was felt asking any pub if a large group of football supporters could be accommodated, and advertising it on email and twitter, wasn't the most sensible idea. We arrived as they opened and obtained a large area in the **Sheaf** and the 50 or so who turned up were well looked after. The large underground pub proved an excellent choice, escaping the bustle of nearby Borough Market. It served Fuller's and Young's beers along with up to 7 other beers.

Who could forget that long range lob from Adam Armstrong, for the first at Millwall that day, as we ran out 4-0 winners? A big thank you should go to Millwall for including, in their match day programme, an article on CCLSC. It was very much appreciated.

After the Millwall game, a number of members were enticed by Rob Stevens to go to a Craft Beer Brewery in Bermondsey. Unfortunately upon arrival, the brewery was closed, despite Rob insisting he had spoken to them beforehand, and been assured they would be open after the game. You couldn't arrange a P up in a brewery jokes abounded.

The following season, talk was of Millwall seeking revenge for the mauling we gave them last time. We followed the same procedure of not advertising our designated pub for our game in September 2016. This time however we did book an area at the Sheaf. This meant we were all together, albeit many having to stand as this time we were sharing a packed pub with TV supporters watching the Manchester derby on the large screens.

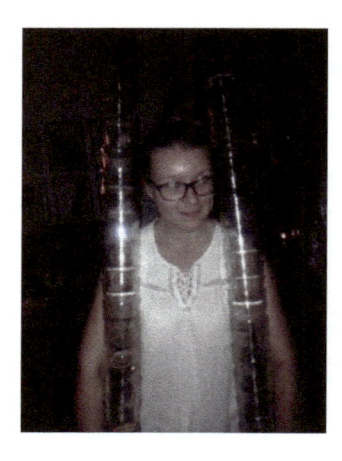

The Assistant manager at the Sheaf pictured clearing glasses from our area. She told me there were 37 empty glasses on this run!

Pictured below on the train from London Bridge are from left to right (back row) Swiss based Andrea and Albi, Norwegian members, Tor and his family, Linda, Sondre and Sebastian, and front row, Joakim, Jorg Erik and Fredrik. Fredrik who says he is a Villa fan did wear his Sky Blues shirt in the ground!

Milton Keynes Dons
Ground – Stadium MK

This is one of the best stadiums we visited in this period. Built in 2007 the facilities are first class, including the big "Emirates style" comfy seats. It has a capacity of 30,000 and they have given generous away allocations, to us and other teams, which has led to memorable away day experiences.

On several visits the Sky Blue Army were out in strength selling out their ticket allocation of up to 8,000 (January 2018). We had the North Stand upper and lower tiers.

Results

29 Dec 2012	3-2	League One	(Moussa, Elliott 2)
30 Nov 2013	3-1	League One	(Dagnall, Maguire 2)
23 Aug 2014	0-0	League One	
18 Mar 2017	0-1	League One	
27 Jan 2018	1-0	FA Cup	(Biamou)
19 Oct 2019	0-0	League One	
03 Dec 2019	0-2	FL Trophy	

The November 2013 game will be remembered for the Sky Blues coming from behind to score three second half goals including the two late goals from free kicks by Chris Maguire.

CCLSC members made a number of welcome returns to the Red Lion, in Fenny Stratford. With several thousands of Sky Blues supporters attending the games against MK Dons in December 2012, November 2013 and August 2014, a packed **Red Lion**, although it didn't serve food, looked after us well. There was a local fish and chip shop in the village and food outlets near the ground.

The Red Lion is a small lock-side pub which is just over a mile from the ground and a couple of minutes walk from Fenny Stratford station. It had a real ale enthusiast landlord and served a rolling choice of three ales, and up to five real ciders.

For the August 2014 game there were planned engineering works around Watford. We therefore travelled from central London via Bedford to Fenny Stratford rather than on the usual quicker inter-city trains direct to Milton Keynes. The good humour amongst the travelling group was evident. Texts were sent to those who were late for the connection at Bedford saying we were in the furthest carriage. As they raced across the bridge to change platforms they discovered it was only a one carriage train! The train stopped at places we had not heard of. The train conductor, having a packed train for once, went out of his way to inform us that if we went down the platform at Fenny Stratford, rather than out the main entrance, it was quicker to the Red Lion.

In March 2017, as a show of appreciation, several members paid tribute to Barry at the Red Lion, with a large thank you banner, for all his work in organising, collecting and distributing our Wembley tickets. Barry's late arrival meant we were able to take a photo without his knowledge.

Barry and Kev Randall had travelled from Nuneaton, and waited at Milton Keynes for the short train journey to Fenny Stratford on London Midland. They somehow got on a Virgin train going north. The first stop was at Lichfield, before having to wait for one hour for the return journey south. They both received a round of applause when they eventually arrived at the Red Lion.

Things were about to change at the Red Lion however. That day we were served beer in plastic glasses for our visit. Many returning after the game, to catch their train from Fenny Stratford, were served their beers in glass pints as the Six

Nations Rugby was shown on the TV screens. The landlord said he now always served football fans in plastic glasses, but not rugby fans, despite agreeing that we had not caused any problems at the Red Lion on our many visits. We vowed never to return.

So the January 2018 FA Cup match against MK Dons may not have been the tie we wanted but the team deserved our support and just under 8,000 turned out to cheer them on. After several years of visiting the Red Lion at Fenny Stratford,  the landlord's attitude towards us and football fans in general on our visit the previous March, meant that we sought a new pub. Tim, the landlord at the **Chequers** in Fenny Stratford, could not have been more different. He opened up early, had seating and pre ordered food ready for us. Perhaps the numbers of our members took both us and him slightly by surprise. He had to stop taking food orders and constantly ran out of glasses, but not beer!

In comparison with some of the other pubs in Fenny Stratford that day, we didn't do that badly. Those arriving later all mention the chaos at nearby pubs (and the plastic glasses once again at the Red Lion). Those waiting for beers in the Chequers formed an orderly queue throughout even though the wait was a long one!

Max Biamou scored the only goal to put the Sky Blues into the next round.

We were next to play against MK Dons in October 2019 and a month later in the League Cup. By then the Chequers had closed its doors but the local branch of CAMRA advised that the **Red Lion** had recently had new landlords and perhaps we should try them again. We did and on our return landlady Karen provided good beers, pre-ordered food and a warm welcome at the canal side pub. A large group, including Dave Evans and his family, an expatriate based in Russia, enjoyed the Wadsworth 6X, Draught Bass and Marston beers that were served in glasses.

We were to return for the midweek Cup game a month later, with vastly reduced numbers. Karen welcomed us again but wanted to know where everyone was!

Morecambe
Ground – Globe Arena

Morecambe moved into the Globe Arena in 2010. It has a capacity of 6,500 and was named after the construction company that built it. It is dominated by the Peter McGuigan stand on one side. Opposite is a very small open terrace. The Sky Blues Army were located in the Beyondradio Away Stand (pictured), with those seated in the Peter McGuigan Stand.

Results
06 Nov 2016   1-1   FA Cup   (Sterry)
09 Dec 2017   0-2   League Two

Pub

We played Morecambe in the FA Cup on a Sunday in November 2016. With the draw only being made a couple of weeks beforehand, train travel costs were extremely high without the benefits of advanced bookings. Together with a Sunday 2pm kick off for TV reasons, the numbers travelling were reduced. Those that did travel met at the **Eric Bartholomew.** This Wetherspoon pub is dedicated to Eric Morecambe (born Eric Bartholomew) and is near the sea front. It served the normal Spoons beers and food. The very large fish and chips were a favourite that day.

Just around the corner from the pub is the statue of Eric Morecambe, set against the backdrop of Morecambe Bay. Those walking along the front at Morecambe certainly had to look far out into the sea for the tide, but many posed for the obligatory photo at the Eric Morecambe statute. As Kev, Barry and I arrived at the statue, a group of tourists were taking their photos. We waited patiently for them to finish. Bracing the freezing wind, we stripped off our coats, for our own photo in our replica shirts, and turning round discovered the tourists were nowhere to be seen. Several minutes later we did get a passerby to take our photo in front of Eric, now wearing a sky blue scarf. Eric seemed happy to wear the scarf but being a lifelong Luton fan, couldn't be persuaded to become a member of the Coventry City London Supporters' Club.

A much larger group travelled to the League Two game in December 2017. Kev, Barry and I recreated the photo at Eric's statue, thirteen months on, before the much larger group photo was taken. The large party travelling by train from London had to change at Lancaster. The schedule only allowed for an 8 minute wait at Lancaster. Trains were then hourly for the 10 minute journey onto Morecambe. The London train was running over 15 minutes late but for once the departure of the train from Lancaster was delayed, and we were all hurried onto the Morecambe bound train as it departed.

Newport County
Ground – Rodney Parade

The ground capacity is reduced to just below 8,000 when County play. The ground is shared with Newport Gwent Dragons who are allowed a capacity of 11,500. The Sky Blue Army were in the Bisley Stand (pictured) and in the temporary stand behind the goal. The South Stand, which only covers about half of the pitch, and where the temporary stand had been erected, has an unusual looking double-decker type of building behind. In the far corner there are the changing rooms under a pyramid shaped roof.

The entrance to the away supporters section is at the opposite end of the stadium to the home areas and is accessed along Corporation Road (so no need to go through the main stadium entrance). It is poorly signposted and is literally a small pathway situated in-between some residential houses.

Results
30 Mar 2018   1-1   League Two   (Biamou)

Max Biamou was to replace Peter Vincenti with 15 minutes to go and scored the equaliser two minutes later.

Pub

The one visit to Newport was on Easter Good Friday in March 2018. CCLSC members met at the **Pen & Wig**, a ten minute walk from the station, although many jumped in taxis to arrive at the pub by noon. It served prodigious amounts of Draught Bass, it being the last bastion of the famous Burton ale which was once common place in the town centre's pubs. The pub was also a strong supporter of Welsh breweries for its other ales.

Amy, and her staff, provided a large food selection for lunch, with those with CCLSC travel or match tickets obtained by CCLSC having pre ordered. Fortunately for us, Newport had played Tottenham Hotspur in the FA Cup a few weeks before and had erected a temporary stand for additional away fans. The Sky Blue Army took the increased allocation.

We were joined that day on the train from Paddington to Newport by Manhattan based Bob and Ash. They had become engaged in Wales and had deliberately booked their trip to coincide with the Newport game, and a return to Wales. Who said romance was dead?

Northampton Town
Ground – Sixfields Stadium (in 2018 it was renamed the PTS Academy Stadium)

For those that didn't venture to Sixfields during our brief exile, or stand on Jimmy's Hill (pictured), the stadium is built on a leisure complex on the outskirts of Northampton. It holds 7,750 and the Sky Blue Army were given 1450 tickets. The away end, behind the goal, holds 800 and the remainder were on the side of the pitch. This stand along the side of the pitch and opposite the Main stand was not fully completed during our exile or at our only away visit. The original plan i understand was that they would incorporate Executive Boxes.

Results
28 Jan 2017   0-3   League One

Manager Russell Slade, before the game, said he wanted to put on a performance for the Sky Blues fans. Once again we travelled in large numbers. It wasn't to be. The return of the unwanted flares and the early sending off meant it was always going to be an uphill struggle, which unfortunately resulted in crowd trouble.

Pub

The Lamplighter, is over 1 mile from the station and 2.8 miles from the ground. It had been recommended by now Northampton based member Lambo, and had been our designated "home pub" during our exile season. Our only visit as an away pub was in January 2017. Paul, the landlord, opened early at 11 am, to accommodate us and over 40 members enjoyed beers from Nene Valley, Oakham and Phipps and Vale. The full English breakfast was popular.

It was a welcome return, or a first time visit for some who had boycotted Sixfields. Paul did us proud by reserving almost all the tables in the main bar. (We did feel for the family, with two small children, who came in for lunch in what is usually a very quiet Saturday lunchtime).

Paul sent me an email afterwards thanking us for keeping him and his staff busy. He added that we certainly enjoyed the beers and to let him know if we are ever heading back in the future. We unfortunately haven't been back since.

Norwich City
Ground – Carrow Road

Copyright Owen Pavey

Carrow Road has a capacity of 27,000 and both ends are two-tiered with a row of Executive Boxes. The large South Stand is a single tier cantilever. The Sky Blue Army were in the corner (pictured thanks to Owen Pavey).

Results
23 Aug 2016   1-6   League Cup   (Lameiras)

Pub

In the good old days of the Championship, when we played at Carrow Road regularly, a favourite meeting place, near the railway station, was the **Coach & Horses.** This coaching inn, with its iconic balcony, is the home of the Chalk Hill Brewery, serving their full range of beers.

Travelling numbers were very limited as the last train back to London that evening departed at 9.15 pm. As a result there was no group travel.

Shown below are Phil, Barry and Sarah with her Dad, Kevin.

Notts County
Ground – Meadow Lane

The ground was completely rebuilt in the 1990s. Meadow Lane is smart and an enjoyable place to watch a game. It's the ground that most resembles the old Highfield Road. It has four separate stands and has a capacity of just over 20,000. The Sky Blue Army were in the Jimmy Sirrel stand (pictured), along the side of the pitch. It has a gable on its roof reminiscent of old grounds.

Results

Date	Score	Competition	Scorers
27 Apr 2013	2-2	League One	(Fleck, Moussa)
08 Feb 2014	0-3	League One	
06 Apr 2015	0-0	League One	
07 Apr 2018	1-2	League Two	(Ponticelli)
18 May 2018	4-1	League Two Play-off	(Biamou 2, McNulty, Bayliss)

Pub

On our visits to Notts County we have enjoyed pre match drinks at the **Canalhouse**, a short walk from the station. The three storey Castle Rock pub has a canal inlet on the inside, traversed by wooded walkways. This unusual pub has a resident narrowboat moored inside the pub! It has a generous canal-side decked patio, which we have used whenever the weather permitted. It served the Castle Rock range of real ale beers and in addition a number of guest beers. It also has probably the largest continental beer range in Nottingham with Belgium, Czech and German beers featuring.

We were to first visit in April 2013 moving from the Fellows next door which we had used in the past. It was much larger, and would accommodate our bigger group travelling, and was cheaper according to Nottingham based Alan Murphy. For our next visit in February 2014 it coincided with a Beer Festival at the Canalhouse. This featured over 50 ales in the upstairs bars. Given the train times back from Nottingham we had time to drown our sorrows after the match, a poor 3-0 defeat.

Pictured are Charles and George sampling the additional beers at the Beer Festival.

In 2015, a large CCLSC following were at a sunny Nottingham for the Easter Monday game, and sat outside on the terrace at the Canalhouse.

We didn't return again until April 2018. Another very sunny day saw Mrs Ogleby and daughter Rachel joining us in Nottingham that day. They had both intended on going shopping whilst we were all at the game. However enjoying the sunny patio and the wine, they were still at the same tables when we returned. Did they ever go shopping?

Mrs O was seen complaining why we were on such an early train back to London. Robin's defence was that we always caught early trains back to see our loved ones, but it didn't cut the mustard!

We were disappointed with a 2-1 defeat, despite substitute Jordon Ponticelli having looked to have secured a dramatic late point. They often say you are most vulnerable just after you have scored. So it was disappointing to concede a goal straight after our equaliser. Had we blown our play-off chances that day we asked on the journey home?

Wayne, the Manager, was looking forward to welcoming us back, after just a few weeks, for the Friday evening Playoff Semi Final, in May. They were busy again with the large number of CCLSC members arriving throughout the afternoon. They were part of the 4,500 Sky Blues supporters that evening. Members pictured in happy mood before the game.

Of course, everyone at the game that evening knows where they were and what they were doing. The 4-1 win was to take us to Wembley. Many had booked hotel rooms in Nottingham as travel back to London that evening was virtually impossible with the last trains leaving at 10 o'clock. This would be a push at ninety minutes but with the possibility of extra time, impossible.

Celebrating in the ground are Martin, Chris and Rob (pictured).

Charles and a few others were back at the Canalhouse after the game and had got the rounds in.

Security on the door would not allow a larger group of us in, many wearing colours. It was due to police advice we were told, and despite loud remonstrations that we had booked an area with Wayne earlier in the day, the security guards wouldn't budge. Phones were buzzing and another group were in the **Company Inn**, a Wetherspoon pub, just around the corner. They had no such security constraints. So off to Spoons it was. The news came through, as we were celebrating and discussing how we would get our tickets for Wembley, that tickets were going on sale the following morning. As I said, many were staying in hotels in Nottingham that night. When last orders were announced, it was only 11pm!

Ye Olde Salutation Inn, a few minutes' walk away, was open until 1 am. We were the only group in this 17th century, Grade II listed, historical, oak beamed, stone floored pub with its labyrinth of caves. It was a music pub with rock bands featuring regularly according to the notice boards. It served a number of real ales in good condition as the conversation continued well past midnight about Biamou's overhead kick and how do we get Wembley tickets. We were all word perfect with the 1,2 3, 4 Michael Doyle song by then!

A military operation of coordinating tickets went in to play the following morning from various hotel rooms or from wherever members had stayed in the local area.

Oldham Athletic
Ground – Boundary Park

It lies at the north western extremity of Oldham, with the towns of Royton and Chadderton lying immediately north and west respectively, giving rise to the name Boundary Park. The capacity is just over 10,600. The Sky Blue Army were in the Caddy Road End (pictured) behind the goal. The look of the ground was improved with the opening in 2015 of the new North Stand, now called the Joe Royle Stand.

Results

29 Sep 2012	1-0	League One	(McDonald)
21 Apr 2014	0-0	League One	
21 Oct 2014	1-4	League One	(Maddison)
08 May 2016	2-0	League One	(Vincelot, Armstrong)
11 Feb 2017	2-3	League One	(Tudgay, Thomas)

Pub

In September 2012 we recommended the **Rose of Lancaster** in Chadderton, which is 200 metres from the Oldham Mills Hill train station. This Lees house is on the canal but is a 30 minute walk to Boundary Park. Jim McIilwaine was one of the few who visited as other travellers going via Manchester went directly to Oldham.

The difficulty of getting to Boundary Park by public transport was slightly eased in 2014. Members travelled via Manchester from Market Street (a short walk from Manchester Piccadilly) to the newly opened Metrolink station, Oldham Central. The designated pub was 100 yards from the Metro station. Big thanks went out to Phil Smith that day, for purchasing the metro tickets for those on the London train, meaning we caught our connection out to Oldham.

The group of members visited the **Ashton Arms**, in the centre of Oldham, before the Easter Monday game. We were treated to their Easter beer festival. All the beers had animal names. When I called and said a dozen or so supporters would be going Jo, the Landlady, said no food would be available but she would put on light sandwich snacks which, at a ridiculously low price of £1.50 each (for those of us who live in the South East), supplemented the range of beers sampled.

We were to return in far smaller numbers for the Tuesday evening fixture in October 2014.

It was the last game of the season, in May 2016, that we next played at Oldham. The Ashton Arms didn't open until 11.30 am on a Sunday and it was not practical for those travelling on the first train out of Euston that morning to partake with the 12.30 kick off.

Steve Pittam, from Dubai, was in the UK for the Oldham game. Steve was meeting his friend John, who is an Arsenal supporter, at Manchester Piccadilly. Despite Arsenal playing in Manchester the same day he was joining Steve at the Oldham match.

Steve offered Chris Anderson, who was also on the Euston train, Adrian Hawthorne and I a lift to the ground. John was pleasantly surprised that the CEO travelled with supporters. That wouldn't happen at a club like Arsenal he added. John was also very impressed with the City support after the "library" which is the Emirates.

Thanks to the lift Adrian and I were able to grab a quick pint with Barry and a group of other members at the **Clayton Green** Brewers Fayre, a couple of minutes walk from the ground. The local CAMRA branch reported later that they had stopped serving real ale in 2017.

We were back at the Ashton Arms in February 2017. As with most northern based games, we were joined by Tony, Adrian and Stuart. Our poor results continued at Oldham, and after another poor defeat, we suffered a horrendous train journey home. Not only were we severely delayed on the way back to Euston but the train was full of Man Utd supporters (well they went to the game and the shop by the looks of it), plus Watford and Palace fans.

Pictured is the very appropriate sign from the Ashton Arms.

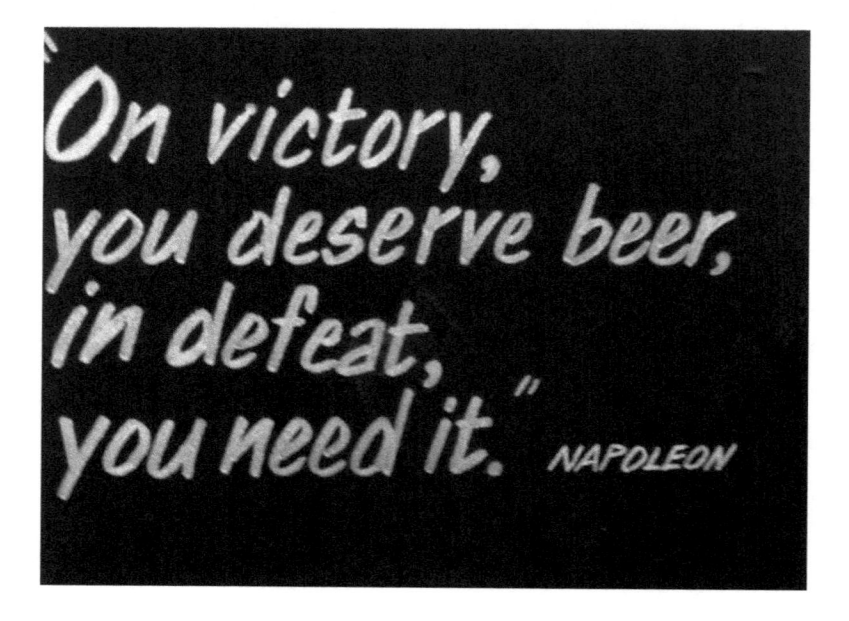

Oxford United
Ground – Kassam Stadium

The Kassam is located on the outskirts of Oxford. It has only three sides, with one end remaining unused, so we watched for wayward shots as they flew into the car park. Each of the stands are of a good size, are all seated, covered and are roughly of the same height. It has a capacity of 12,500. The Sky Blue Army were in one side of the North Stand, where the view and leg room are good.

Results

Date	Score	Competition	Scorers
27 Jul 2013	0-1	Friendly	
19 Nov 2016	1-4	League One	(Tudgay)
14 Aug 2018	0-2	League Cup	
09 Sep 2018	2-1	League One	((og), Chaplin)
31 Aug 2019	3-3	League One	(Westbrooke, Godden, O'Hare)

Oxford railway station is over four miles from the stadium and it is not advisable to walk. A taxi was our preferred transport from the station to the stadium. However, the service on our visits was best described as terrible on several occasions. You can also get the Oxford Bus Service, number 5, from the station to the stadium which we had to use in an emergency. On all of our visits there was heavy traffic after the game. The journey back into the city centre always seemed to take longer than planned.

Pub

The Sky Blues hadn't played in Oxford since 1988 when a few members went to the pre season friendly in July 2013. We met at the CAMRA Good Beer Guide pub, the **Royal Blenheim,** a street corner Victorian pub in the city centre. It was owned by Everards, but leased to White Horse as their Brewery Tap.

In November 2016 we returned to the Royal Blenheim (pictured). It still served the full range of White Horse beers alongside one Everards' beer as part of their 10 handpumps. It was still in the CAMRA Good Beer Guide.

One other note of interest was that the Blenheim didn't show soccer on its several TVs, apparently only rugby and American Football. However, Mick and Jane did welcome us as they said we sounded like a "proper bunch of football supporters" in response to my email when contacting them.

The kick off times at future games meant we went elsewhere.

For the evening Cup game in August 2018 it was not possible to get back into London or other areas of the South of England by train after the match. We met at **Seven Stars on the Green,** Marsh Baldon, just off the M40. This old coaching inn reopened

as a community pub in 2013, and is next to the village green. We chose this pub on the outskirts of Oxford because every member who obtained tickets through CCLSC was travelling by car, due to the nonexistent public transport after the game. This also made sense given the lack of parking in Central Oxford and the distance to the Kassam stadium from the city centre.

Matt the landlord, welcomed us on what was a beautiful summer evening. His staff ensured food orders were taken before the kitchen opened at 6pm, knowing we would be leaving for the game, some four miles away by 7 pm. It served two regular beers, Fullers and Loose Cannon with two changing beers typically from Lodden, Shotover Trinity or White Horse breweries. This was a superb pub with excellent beer (for those not driving).

The following month, September 2018, the sun was again out for the Sunday noon kick off due to Sky TV. CCLSC members did not meet officially for pre match drinks given the midday start time. Those arriving earlier enough into Oxford by train did grab a quick drink in the city centre at **St Aldates Tavern**. It was a much better performance, and the first away win of the season 2-1. We had booked three mini bus taxis but with everyone else's taxis being late arriving at the ground, another group of

Coventry fans tried, unsuccessfully, to jump into one of our taxis. In the confusion one of our minibus' left with a spare seat and with the final one delayed due to traffic; it meant we were one seat short. Alastair Laurie set off to catch a bus and actually walked back along the bypass passing one of the mini buses in the stationary traffic. Post match drinks back at the St Aldates were highly recommended.

We therefore went to the St Aldates Tavern, in August 2019. Monika reserved an area for our group, which didn't please the "local" Man Utd fans arriving to watch them for the TV game that lunchtime. This city centre old coaching inn served up to four real ales, with CAMRA discount available for these. Unfortunately, with several beers running out that day and the limited choice of food available left something to be desired. It was a crazy 3-3 draw, with both sides scoring in time added on and the CCLSC Player of the Season, Fankaty Dabo, scoring two own goals. Dabo was the Oxford top scorer at the end of August!

After the game our pre booked taxis did not arrive to pick us up. We decided it was the bus back into town. Our patience at the bus stop by the ground finally got the better of us. Our group following Rob Stevens walked around the ground into the adjacent housing estate to eventually get a bus back into Oxford. It meant by the time we had travelled back into Oxford, we had missed our train. Fortunately, GWR honoured our tickets on the next London bound service.

Peterborough United
Ground – London Road (in 2019 it was renamed Weston Homes Stadium)

Copyright Joe Dent

The Sky Blue Army have more recently been in the Motorpoint Stand behind the goal (photo looking towards the away end thanks to John Dent). Our earlier visits were in the terrace behind the goal and whilst the new stand was being built accommodated along the half way line. With all the redevelopment the capacity is now just over 15,000.

Results

12 Apr 2014	0-1	League One	
28 Mar 2015	1-0	League One	(Tudgott)
25 Mar 2016	1-3	League One	(Cole)
31 Dec 2016	1-1	League One	(Willis)
16 Mar 2019	2-1	League One	(Bakayoko, Enobakhare)
26 Oct 2019	2-2	League One	(Bakayoko, Biamou)

For the 2016 Good Friday game we were joined on the train journey from Kings Cross to Peterborough by Danes Per, Jesper and a couple of their friends, and Norwegians Roar and Steinar. Then Finland resident and Coventry expat Dave Evans joined us with his family at the Brewery Tap. They all enjoyed the beer, if not the result

Pub

The pub of choice for the almost annual visit to play the Posh was the **Brewery Tap**. The Tap is reputed to be the largest brewpub in Europe, housed in the former Labour Exchange. It is a couple of minutes walk from the station, and is the home of a custom-made specialist brew plant for Oakham Ales, which can be viewed through a glass wall. It serves up to twelve real ales on tap and bottled Belgian beers. Excellent, good-value Thai food is served and this spacious pub has a mix of comfortable leather sofas with low tables together with tables and chairs for diners.

General Manager Jessica Loock, in April 2014, said that the Tap would be big enough to cater for our size of group and looked forward to seeing us. Barry Chattaway and his group returned after the game, saying he had left his mobile phone there. A pitiful excuse if you ask me!

It was a return to the Brewery Tap in March 2015, with its excellent Oakham Ales and Thai food. Numbers were slightly down on the previous season's visit, due to holidays, a golden wedding anniversary and a Committee member's wedding taking place that day. Congratulations from all at CCLSC went to Barry and Val for reaching such a milestone and we wished Jay and Rachel all the very best in their future married life together.

December 31, 2016 again saw us return to the Brewery Tap which continued to be our regular pub of choice and gave a unique experience, coupling authentic Thai cuisine with its Oakham ales, including Citra, JHB and Inferno.

The members missed the Brewery Tap in our League Two season and the fixtures meant we were to return twice in 2019. In the March, train times meant we were outside the Tap before opening. Some members, rather than wait, went to the nearby **Ostrich Inn** before returning to the Brewery Tap for the beers and Thai food.

What a brilliant atmosphere the SBA created at Peterborough that day. The Sky Blues Army was singing from start to finish in support of the team. The reception at the end reminded many of the Notts County game. The players rewarded the supporters with a top class performance. The late deflection saw Posh score but the 2-1 score line flattered Peterborough.

Peterborough scored in the last minute again in December. It was a much more assured City performance this time, with the home team top of the table going into the game. The media felt we were the better footballing side. Of course, League One doesn't have Video Assistant Referee (VAR), but like most supporters at Premier League games, the SBA had absolutely no idea why Bakayoko's "goal" hadn't been given. The disallowed goal, for handball, on the TV highlights afterwards, clearly showed that it was the defender and not Bakayoko who had handled it. There was no need for VAR for Max Biamou's goal. He only seems to score fantastic goals. It was a shame that the last kick of the game allowed Peterborough to equalise.

Having enjoyed the Ostrich Inn the previous March, trains were arranged to arrive into Peterborough before the Tap opened so we could sample their beers again.

Plymouth Argyle
Ground – Home Park

There was re-development and refurbishment work ongoing when we visited (The main Grandstand was reopened in January 2020). Once completed the capacity of Home Park would be 18,000. The Sky Blue Army were in the Barn Park Stand behind the goal (picture is looking towards the Barn Park Stand). The close proximity to the home fans did lead to good humoured banter.

Results
19 Jan 2019   1-2   League One   (Chaplin)

Pub

There was a larger than expected group who travelled to Plymouth in January 2019. This was our first visit since the Championship days. We visited a new pub, the **Fortescue Hotel**, about a 20 minute walk from the station and just under 2 miles from the ground. The pub was the 2018 Local CAMRA Branch Pub of the Year and served up to 9 real ales, including regulars Bays Devon Dumpling, Skinner's Betty Stogs and St Austell Proper Job. CAMRA members obtained discount on real ales. Food was not available at lunchtimes but Tasha informed me that there are plenty of takeaway places around the pub and we could bring food in to enjoy with our pint(s).

Plymouth is the most westerly and southerly league ground in England. Several members decided to make a weekend of the long trip, including Phil Higgins who knew Plymouth from his Royal Navy days. Phil is pictured with Scott Harbertson, along with Barry and son, Matt.

For those not staying over it was 10 hour travelling that day for two hours in the pub and 90 minutes of football, losing 2-1.

Earlier that January saw Mark Robins and Dave Boddy attend an evening Q&A at the Calthorpe Arms, in Central London. Dave and Mark had been trying to get down to London to see us for some time. The wait didn't disappoint. Everyone found their candour over subjects that we are all concerned about refreshing and no one could fail to be optimistic about the future on the pitch after listening to Mark's philosophies and the passion he has to succeed in the right way for the long term benefit of the club. Congratulations went to the raffle winners Rob Stevens, Paul Stokes, Claire Mellon and Brian Klitzner. The proceeds from the evening were donated to the Family Zone, and Treasurer, Kevin Randall, presented a cheque to Pat Raybould at half time at the Plymouth game.

Portsmouth
Ground – Fratton Park

Fratton Park is a decaying relic of a ground, and all the more enjoyable for it. It holds just over 21,000. On our visits there was normally a great atmosphere with 'The Pompey Chimes' song sung by Portsmouth fans usually aided by the somewhat irritating drummer and bell ringer in the Fratton End. Originating in the 1890s it is thought to be the world's oldest football chant still in use. The Sky Blue Army were in one side of the Milton End (pictured) which is a former terrace with seats bolted on and a couple of pillars to get in the way of the game. Facilities are pretty basic and no alcohol is served in the away end. Despite several seasons in League One and one season in League Two, and visiting many new grounds, the away end at Portsmouth still has the worst toilets seen since those at the old Colchester ground.

Results

23 Mar 2013	0-2	League One	
21 Jul 2015	1-2	Friendly	(Thomas)
22 Apr 2019	1-2	League One	(Hiwala)
20 Aug 2019	3-3	League One	(Hiwala, Godden, Rose)

Pub

We met at another good real ale pub before the Portsmouth game in March 2013. The **Artillery Arms**, serving up to five cask ales, welcomed the CCLSC members with a BBQ, which was only reserved for the "big" games, rather than just pies. Unfortunately, with the poor weather that day the BBQ had to be cooked inside in the kitchen.

There was a pre season friendly in 2015. The game was played at the ground of Havant & Waterlooville. Before the game we met at the **Old House at Home,** which served Fuller's, Gales and guest beers. It was a short walk from Havant station.

We were joined by a Coventry fan that night who admitted he hasn't seen the team much lately. Alastair Laurie recalls he was clearly enthusiastic and knowledgeable about City. John Bains recalls that Carl Lawton was making a number of signs behind his back to me when I mentioned CCLSC. It transpired he had spent some time at Her Majesty Pleasure. He never did join.

The teams did not meet at Fratton Park again until Easter Monday April 2019. The game was an early kick off as it was televised on Sky TV. We saw a very good performance at Portsmouth which ultimately saw us lose 2-1. CCLSC members did grab a quick pint beforehand at the **John Jacques** in Fratton Road. Locally based member, John Bains, ensured that any members challenged by security at the entrance mentioned they were guests of John's firm. A large number of members met after the game back at the Artillery Arms.

Michael Moore, from Australia, joined us for the first time at the Portsmouth match. Michael pictured, with the scarf and nearest the camera, with a group of members at the Artillery Arms after the game.

It was one of those "I was there moments" for anyone at Pompey for the evening game in August 2019. The spirit and fight, which was to result in promotion later in the season, was evident as we came back from 3-1, when down to nine men, to earn the draw, with Michael Rose's late equaliser. Several of the regular travellers booked overnight hotel accommodation. Meeting in the **Brewhouse & Kitchen** mid afternoon we enjoyed the Mucky Duck and Mary Rose Brewhouse beers with a late lunch/early dinner. Taking taxis across Portsmouth to the Artillery Arms we met a large contingent of southern based CCLSC members assembled in the large garden before and after the game, where we were made welcome once again.

Our only Cayman Islands member over the years, Mark White, who had recently retired and returned to the UK is pictured here with me in the garden at the Artillery Arms. Mark, who joined as a UK member was to see a number of games with us that season

.

Port Vale
Ground – Vale Park

The ground is located in the town of Burslem, one of the six towns comprising Stoke-on-Trent. Longport station is the closest to the ground, but is a good 30 minute walk away and is not well served by trains, compared with Stoke-on-Trent.

Vale Park with its capacity of 19,000 has a good mixture of the old and the new but is let down overall by the fact that the Lorne Street Stand, was not fully completed on our visits. This stand which is two-tiered has a row of executive boxes situated between its large lower tier and smaller upper tier.

The Sky Blues Army were located in the Hamil Road end (pictured). Up to 4,500 away supporters can be accommodated in the Signal One Stand (Hamil Road was on the back of the tickets!), where the view and facilities located in the concourse behind the stand is good. The often large SBA really made some noise from this stand, as the acoustics are excellent. However, the slope is quite shallow, which might affect your view should a tall person be seated in front. The view is very good generally, although there are 4 supporting pillars that can get in the way if you are more than half way back. Port Vale were one of several Club's who regularly applied UNRESERVED seating. This was very annoying as we would spend time and effort organising for CCLSC members to be seated together.

The pitch is one of the widest in the League and the crowd is further set back from the playing action by the surrounding cinder track.

If you wonder at half time why the Port Vale fans seem transfixed with staring at the away end, it is not intimidation, but the electric scoreboard perched on the roof of this stand! (the away fans can't see the scoreboard).

Results

21 Sep 2013	2-3	League One	(Wilson, Moussa)
13 Dec 2014	2-0	League One	(Johnson, Madine)
07 Feb 2016	1-1	League One	(Murphy)
01 Oct 2016	2-0	League One	(Sordell, McCann)
26 Dec 2017	0-1	League Two	

The October 2016 game was two days after Tony Mowbray's resignation and was Mark Venus' first game in caretaker charge.

Pub

Most, if not all of us travelling by train ended up at Stoke-on-Trent railway station, which is over four miles away. Pre booked taxis from the station to the designated pub, the **Bull's Head**, situated in the centre of Burslem, worked well, if sometimes they were a little delayed.

The Bull is Titanic's brewery tap flagship pub. The range of real ales is complemented by a good selection of real ciders and bottled Belgian beers. Bob, the landlord, always responded to our email about our next visit by saying, "I was waiting for your email". There was a pre match BBQ at all Vale home games and the "Match Day Special" double cheese and bacon burger along with the full range of Titanic beers proved very popular with the CCLSC members.

We hadn't played Port Vale since March 1964 in the old Division Three, so a large group travelled to Port Vale in September 2013. We were joined by SBI members Mark White, from the Cayman Islands, and Morten Moen from Norway. With the Sky Blues playing at Northampton that season and battle lines being drawn, it appeared there was no light at the end of the tunnel between the various factions; Mark constantly had to deny he had any Cayman connections with our owners!

Bob opened early at 11 am for the early 2pm Sunday kick off in February 2016, which saw a smaller group than normal at the Bulls Head. We were joined by SBI member, Hannu Solanne (pictured below with the hat) from Finland. It was his second visit of the season having been over to the Wigan and Rochdale games at the start of the season.

It was another welcome return to the Titanic Brewery pub, the Bulls Head, before the Port Vale game in October 2016. "If only the Titanic had been Sky Blue..." and other old jokes were recalled, but saw our group in good humour before the game. Several members signed a "Thank You" card for Tony Mowbray at the Bulls Head. Many recalling the excellent attacking football we had played under his stewardship.

Despite no public transport for the Boxing Day game in 2017, Barry ordered 25 tickets for CCLSC members, many of whom met at the Bulls Head before the game on our last visit. Pictured below are Sara, Barry, Lambo and Christian and his son.

Preston North End
Ground - Deepdale

Three sides of the stadium are composed of some excellent looking all seater stands, complete with some spectacular looking floodlights. They are of the same height and style and are all large, covered, single tiered stands. Each has a likeness of a past player outlined on the seats. The fourth stand is the Invincibles Stand (named after the legendary Preston team of 1888/89). Deepdale has a capacity of 23,400.

The Sky Blue Army were in the modern Bill Shankly Kop at one end of the pitch. It's very steep so there were no problems with the view, especially as there are no pillars to get in the way.

Results

26 Jan 2013	2-2	League One	(Clarke, Robertson, (og))
18 Jan 2014	1-1	League One	(Moussa)
07 Feb 2015	0-1	League One	

We have travelled to Preston on three occasions and always in late January or early February.

Pub

In our first season in League One, we played Preston in January 2013; and met at the **Old Black Bull,** a Mock-Tudor city centre pub. There was no food but it served a good range of real ales and was a previous CAMRA Pub of the Year winner. It was conveniently placed on the way to the ground. It is about a 5 minute walk from the station, opposite St George's Shopping Centre, and is then a 20 minute walk to Deepdale.

For our visit in January 2014 we went to the nearby **Black Horse,** mainly because it did food. It is identified by CAMRA as one of Britain's Best Real Heritage Pubs. Up to eight Robinson's beers are regularly on, including Dizzy Blonde and Old Tom. Upstairs

was the Graze and Grog cafe, serving home-made food, and available in the pub.

Having called beforehand to ensure that they would have food on Saturday lunchtime, we were initially somewhat put out upon arrival to be informed that no food was available. Having mentioned to the guy behind the bar we had called ahead, the landlord came over and explained that the owner from the Café upstairs, which provided the pub food, had been ill since Thursday and won't be open. He did allow us to bring food from MacDonald's and Greggs into the Parlour Bar, which we had made our own.

It was this game that had that goal. Sky Sports News picked it as their Goal of the Day and standing behind the goal seeing Franck Moussa's shot in the 90+6 minutes fly into the net to make it 1-1 certainly made the long journey back on the Virgin train from Preston to Euston much more enjoyable.

The following season, in February 2016, Graham and Angela, the landlords at the Black Horse were away on holiday so they advised there would be limited or no food available. But Paula, who I spoke to, said we could bring food into the pub from outside. She reserved one of the small front rooms for us!

The small group of members who travelled up to Preston that day had a nightmare journey coming home. The train was delayed at Warrington for 90 minutes. What made it worse was that a much larger group of Bournemouth supporters had got on the train at the previous stop, Wigan. They took great delight in telling us how well Callum Wilson was playing, that he was scoring for fun, and what a steal he was at the price they paid for him!

Rochdale
Ground – Crown Oil Arena (known as Spotland)

In 2016 Spotland was renamed the Crown Oil Arena in a five year corporate sponsorship deal. It is traditional but comfy with a decent view. Three sides of Spotland are now all seating with only the Sandy Lane end still terracing. It has a capacity of just over 10,000. The Sky Blues Army were in the Willbutt Lane Stand, pictured, along the side of the pitch.

Results

Date	Score	Competition	Scorers
20 Sep 2014	0-1	League One	
11 Aug 2015	1-1	League Cup	(Tudgay)
20 Oct 2015	0-0	League One	
17 Apr 2017	0-2	League One	
09 Feb 2019	1-0	League One	(Hiwala)
22 Feb 2020	2-1	League One	(Rose, Godden)

Rochdale famously beat Coventry City from Division One (Premier League today) in the FA Cup in 1971. We lost to them in the FA Cup again in 2003 when we were the Premier League team! Even in the League Cup tie in 2015 which ended in a 1-1 draw, we were to lose on penalties with Ruben Lameiras missing. Historically it was not the best place to play.

Pub

In September 2014 we played Rochdale in the league for the first time since 1991. So being a new ground for many, our large group of members went to the **Cemetery Hotel**. From the station the Cemetery is 1.4 miles or a 30 minute walk, so again taxis proved the best bet.

The ground is a 10 minute walk from the pub.

Yes, all the amusing stories came out, see you old folk at the cemetery, see we are meeting in the dead centre of Rochdale, and don't forget your shovel! The Cemetery Hotel, which was a new pub for CCLSC, proved a hit. It had three separate rooms off the main bar area, which did mean we were dispersed throughout the pub. Four real ales were available. The Cemetery is recognised by CAMRA as having a nationally important historic pub interior for its Edwardian decor.

Let's dispel all notions of gloom straight away. The Cemetery Hotel, although right opposite Rochdale's vast cemetery, was actually a cheerful and welcoming sort of place.

It's a home from home for Rochdale Football Club supporters on match days – one room is a shrine to the Dale, with signed shirts and historic photos of rare past triumphs on display. Natalie says that away fans often turn up for friendly pre and post-match analysis, banter and a few pints. It was another football-friendly pub that seems the ideal place to find real ale and civilised company.

A few members returned to the Cemetery in August 2015, for the League Cup defeat, and again in October for the league encounter. Pre booked taxis to and from Rochdale station proved invaluable.

Trains from Manchester Victoria take 15 to 20 minutes out to Rochdale. You can also travel by the Metrolink tram from central Manchester to Rochdale Interchange in just under an hour. This became important for the Easter Monday April 2017 game. That April would see us win at Wembley, get relegated, and the Club's U18 side crowned Professional Development League South Champions.

After the expense of Wembley, a reduced number travelled on Easter Monday. However the top 5 travellers that season, Adrian Hawthorne, Kev Randall, Barry Chattaway, Jim Mcilwaine and myself were at The Cemetery before the game. Trains that day were running on a reduced service which meant we had to catch a very early train from Rochdale to be back to Manchester Victoria, dash across central Manchester to Piccadilly station, to catch our trains back south.

There was a poor performance at Rochdale that day, where at that point we had never won, and relegation was becoming inevitable. We had arranged for a taxi to be at the bottom of Willbutts Lane at 5.05pm. Fortunately, the taxi was waiting and we made the train.

Nobody said following the Sky Blues is easy! Not for the first time several members questioned their sanity as they set off around 7 am to travel to Rochdale on a cold windy winter day in February 2019. Although the proposed Northern Rail train strike had been called off, the train operator couldn't reinstall the full timetable. So from Manchester, instead of a 15 minute train journey, it was nearly an hour on the Metrolink. Advance train tickets meant a minibus back into Manchester after the game, to ensure everyone caught the train back to London.

If all that wasn't bad enough the Virgin train from Euston, earlier that morning, was cancelled. Fortunately, everyone arrived early enough to catch an alternative train north.

This Rochdale trip, after all the travel difficulties, will be one talked about for some time and has entered CCLSC folklore.

Travelling out by the Metrolink meant a new pub. The **Baum** was a 10 minute walk from the Metrolink station according to Google maps. However, it looked to be just the other side of a large shopping centre. A number of us decided  we would walk through the centre rather than follow the Google directions. On first appearance, this looked to be a good decision. Immediately upon entering the shopping centre Google reduced the walking time to the pub to 2 minutes.

Now those who recall the Father Ted episode, where the group of clergy cannot find their way out of the lingerie department, will have a sense of what happened next. As we approached the far exit, Google suddenly increased time to the pub back to 10 minutes. We saw another exit to the right, so off we went only to be informed that the time to the pub hadn't decreased.

Frustrated we reluctantly asked a security guard how to get to the pub. He advised going up the lift to the management services department and if we exited to the car park there we would see the pub. Upon reaching the car park we could see a number of exits. We walked to the one directly opposite, only to find ourselves back in the shopping centre. Turning round we found us back in the car park and from this vantage point we could indeed see the pub.

So slightly later than planned several, by now thirsty, members eventually arrived at the pub. Those already there, all had similar stories of walking for several minutes only to discover they had parked their car in the car park opposite the pub, or had been directed to the other side of the ring road.

All ended well as the range of beers were exceptional and those who tried the local "rag pudding" for lunch were left well satisfied. A little bit of history was made that day. It was the first victory in ten visits over 99 years.

It was to be one of our last away games, in February 2020, when a large group returned to the Baum. It served up to 6 real ales and offers CAMRA discount on its real ales. It is a former CAMRA National Pub of the Year and is just off St Mary's Gate. Dan, the landlord, was to set aside tables for us again. Those who visited last season were raving about the "rag pudding" lunch! The Baum is in the heritage area of Rochdale and next door to the Rochdale Pioneers Museum. Upon arrival, no area had been set aside for us. Dan had not past on the message as he had something more important on his mind. He hadn't been in work all week as his partner had just given birth. We were able to establish ourselves in the conservatory area (pictured), so no harm was done.

A 2-1 win at Rochdale that day, which over the years hasn't been a very successful venue, made it five wins in a row. This was another record broken in a record breaking season. We never score from corners was also put to bed. A clever short corner, following a decoy run by Callum O'Hare, saw a great cross from Liam Walsh to the back post for Michael Rose to head home. The early goal probably didn't help us as Rochdale were to have more possession against us than most teams that season. Much of their possession was passing across their back four, and caused us little or no problems. Matty Godden added a second. That was game over or so we thought. Straight from the kick off a long 'hoof' went in between defenders and keeper for Rochdale to score. As was now our custom, we saw out the game for the three points.

Before the February 2020 game, SBI member Dave Evans, by now living and working in Russia (far right) joined us with his son at the Baum. Martin from Denmark (left), who was joined by three colleagues, had visited Old Trafford for a ground tour that morning. Like Jesper Boss, also from Denmark (centre), who had travelled from Euston with our group suffering the train disruptions, was going to the Arsenal game at the Emirates the following day with friends. They were not certain

whether the Theatre of Dreams or the Emirates would match up to the "real" football and passion of following the Sky Blues on an away day to Spotlands.

Rotherham United
Ground – AESSEAL New York Stadium

The New York Stadium was opened in July 2012 and has a 12,000 capacity with the option of expansion. It is one of the grounds that Tim Fisher has quoted as an example of how any "new" ground in the Coventry area might be like. Unlike most new stadiums which are situated out of town, often in the middle of nowhere, the New York Stadium is close to the town centre and a ten minute walk from the railway station.

The Sky Blue Army were in the Mears Stand behind the goal (photo is looking towards the away end). The angle of the Stand is quite steep and it is a hike to the top. As you would expect from a newish stadium there are good views and facilities.

Results
01 Jan 2014   3-1   League One   (Baker 2, Christie)
05 Oct 2019   0-4   League One

Pub

 It was certainly an early start on New Year's Day for those travelling from the South East to Rotherham in January 2014. I hadn't been to Rotherham, since the old Millmoor days, and we laughed at my directions to the pub from the station. You could see the **Bridge Inn** as you come out of the station!

It was in the 2014 CAMRA Good Beer Guide and was an Old Mill tied house, built in 1930 using stone from the original Bridge Inn dating back to the 1700s. It served Old Mill Traditional Bitter and Yorkshire Porter along with regular guest beers. Being New Years Day the traditional Yorkshire pie and peas was available but not other food. CCLSC members were made welcome as they settled in the large room off the main bar.

Geraldine, in the white hat and scarf above, the daughter of regular traveller Jim McIlwaine joined us that day. She was by then living in France and was persuaded to join the SBI. She was joined by her good friend, the football-loving Finnish Hammer (her words not mine - because she supports West Ham). The Finnish Hammer had been to one Coventry game with Geraldine before, the Man Utd League Cup win at Old Trafford in 2007. She was to see another win, 3-1.

In May later that year, and of course after the season had ended, I was on holiday in Grenada and whilst sitting in the pool bar got speaking to another English couple. It proved what a small world we live in. Our discussion, obviously, got round to football. He was a Rotherham fan. I mentioned I had seen Rotherham play Coventry at three different grounds, Millmoor, Don Valley Stadium in Sheffield and had been to the New York Stadium that January. I mentioned our pre match drink at the Bridge Inn. It was his usual pub before games he said. He remembered the New Year's Day game and specifically not being able to sit with his friends in their usual area to enjoy their pre match pint. It was unusual that away fans had been allowed into the pub he said. I added that it was me who had spoken to the landlord beforehand. Being New Year's Day, the landlord had apparently assumed only a few, not thirty plus, would be arriving from the London Supporters Club when granting permission. Our numbers were further swelled by a number of northern based supporters who by now regularly joined us for pre match drinks at games in the north.

Our next visit was to see one of our only three defeats in the promotion season 2019/20. In October 2019 the Bridge Inn was advertising a no away fans policy so members went to a new pub the **Cutlers Arms**, before the Rotherham game. Interestingly, as we walked past the Bridge Inn there was a bill board  outside saying "AWAY FANS WELCOME". The Cutlers Arms is Grade ll listed and included in CAMRA's National Inventory of Pub Interiors. It offered the full range of Chantry beers and Mick, the landlord, had up to 12 handpumps with all his real ale at £2.70 a pint.

 They regularly had a mix of away and home fans before a game in what he described as a friendly atmosphere. There were no formal meals but snacks such as pickled eggs and pork pies were available. We were made very welcome, but their lack of hot food meant several members arrived later than planned, having eaten at the local Wetherspoon pub first. The area we had reserved had by then been occupied by several locals. We shared the area with them.

Scunthorpe United
Ground – Glanford Park (renamed Sands Venue Stadium in 2019)

This was the first of the generation of new grounds in this country when it was opened in 1988. It is somewhat box like in appearance with all four stands being an equal height. The ground is totally enclosed with all four corners having been filled (with advertising hoardings). The home end is terracing, whilst the other three sides of the ground are seated. It has a capacity of 9,000. The Sky Blue Army were in the South Stand behind the goal (pictured)

Results

09 Mar 2013	2-1	League One	(Baker, Clarke)
16 Sep 2014	1-2	League One	(Nouble)
12 Sep 2015	0-1	League One	
30 Apr 2017	1-3	League One	(Gadzhev)
05 Jan 2019	1-2	League One	(Chaplin)

It has not been a successful of grounds for the Sky Blues. We were leading 1-0 in September 2014 when Reda Johnson was sent off in the 24th minute, and we eventually lost 2-1.

It was a school boy error by Johh Fleck that led to the only goal in 2015.

Pub

The CCLSC members first went to the **Honest Lawyer**, a small pub with *The Gallows Restaurant* above in March 2013. The Honest Lawyer sounds like an oxymoron, but was a superb public house, only 5 minutes walk from the railway station.

In March 2013 there were a good choice of real ales, and the bar food was very good value, London based local Andy Skeels who travelled with us had been a season ticket holder at Glanford Park for 25 years but the Sky Blues have been his 'second' team since he was a schoolboy in Scunthorpe in the 1970s. After moving to London, he became a CCLSC member in the mid-eighties after getting accosted by Chris Lambert (Lambo) in a pub in Central London one night while wearing a Coventry scarf!

It was trains, buses and automobiles to get to Scunthorpe that Saturday. London to Doncaster by train and then there was a train replacement bus service from Doncaster to Scunthorpe. Andy arranged for a number of CCLSC members to have lifts in friends' cars from the Honest Lawyer to the ground, over two miles away from the pub. An interesting aside was that the bus replacement service got us to both Scunthorpe and after the game back to Doncaster before the scheduled train times.

With the evening game in September 2014, in accordance with our policy to meet close to the ground, we met at the

Berkeley Hotel, a 5 minutes walk from the ground. This 1930s Samuel Smith's hotel is identified by CAMRA as one of Britain's Real Heritage Pubs. This proved to be a good choice with its Sam Smith's beer and its historical Art Deco interiors.

 Twelve month later in September 2015, it was another early start for the journey up to Scunthorpe where a larger than anticipated group joined us at the Berkeley Hotel. The Sam Smith's beer was £1.80 per pint and Shane and Theresa welcomed us back to this roomy Samuel Smith's pub.

On our next visit, in April 2017, the final game of the season had a noon kick off. The few CCLSC members making the trip and wanting a beer before the game met at the Wetherspoon pub the **Blue Bell.** This Town Centre pub was over 1.8 miles from the ground but opened at 8.30 am for those long distance supporters travelling. It served the Wetherspoons' usual range of real ales and food. Our usual pub, the Sam Smith's Berkeley Hotel, despite being a 5 minute walk from the ground, was not being allowed to open before midday. So despite its proximity we couldn't visit this time for pre match drinks.

Regular visitor Steve Pittam, from Dubai, and Roy Ebbesen, from Norway, were at Scunthorpe that Sunday. Both had booked flights etc months before thinking it might be an important  end of season game. The 3-1 defeat confirmed relegation.

Roy is shown centre with Barry, and a friend who is a Luton Town support. They had been to see Luton the day before.

A large group travelled up in January 2019. Given the train times several members arrived before noon and visited the Honest Lawyer, which opened at 11 am but by now didn't do food at lunchtime. Our WhatsApp group kept everyone informed when we moved onto the Berkeley Hotel. I had mentioned to the group travelling up by train that the Sam Smiths beers at the Berkeley were £1.80 a pint on our last visit. I got a lot a stick from the group when they found out they were now £2 a pint!

Sheffield United
Ground – Bramall Lane

Bramall Lane, with a capacity of 32,000 is balanced, with all four stands being the same height. The construction of three large modern looking stands, plus the filling in of the corners (albeit one corner is filled with administrative offices), makes it a great ground and one that has character and a unique appearance – a proper ground with a great atmosphere. The Sky Blues Army were in the Redbrik Estate Agency (aka Bramell Lane) stand, pictured, behind one of the goals.

Results

01 Feb 2013	2-1	League One	(Clarke 2)
03 May 2014	1-2	League One	(Delfouneso)
21 Feb 2015	2-2	League One	(Samuel 2)
13 Dec 2015	0-1	League One	
05 Apr 2017	0-2	League One	

The first week in February 2013 started so well with a 2-1 win on a cold Friday evening at Sheffield United, with Leon Clarke scoring a late winner.

Pub

The few CCLSC members at the **Sheaf View**, like on previous trips to Sheffield, found this pub to be friendly even though it is frequented with Blades fans. It had featured on the Championship list of pubs on the CCLSC website for a few years. It had 10 plus ales on offer and is a winner of many CAMRA branch awards. Bramall Lane is about a 10 minute walk away.

Our final game of the season, in May 2014, saw us at the **Devonshire Cat,** where we enjoyed a large range of real ales and good wholesome pub food. With its 12 handpumps adorning the bar and over 100 beers from around the world, the Dev Cat was a great place for the discerning drinker. The menu ranged from light snacks to hearty meals. Manager Brett Starkey opened at 11:30am. The Dev Cat is a 10-15 minute walk from the station and about the same to the ground.

We returned in February 2015 to the Dev Cat. The group was a little smaller than for our visit for the last game of the previous season but we were all in good spirits before the game. It was a couple of minutes of madness that saw a comfortable 2-0 lead disappear, with late goals, including one from Michael Doyle. Manager, Steve Pressley was sacked two days after this game.

Later that year in December 2015 the Sunday game was
shown live on Sky Sports. With the early Sunday lunchtime

kick off at noon there was no group travel from London for this game.

The first train out of London on Sunday morning didn't arrive into Sheffield until 11.50 am. Despite the limited train service on Sunday a small number of members, using other means of transport, did meet at the **Sheffield Tap** at Sheffield Station. Several London based members, who couldn't get to the match due to the early kick off and lack of trains, met in central London at the Sheaf to watch the game together on TV.

For the evening game in April 2017, the few members who travelled returned again to the Devonshire Cap. The Dev Cat, by now operated by Abbeydale Brewery, served 6 of their beers and a number of interesting guest beers. The curse of the former player saw Leon Clarke and John Fleck score the goals that night.

Pictured are Jim, Kev and Barry in the ground.

Shrewsbury Town
Ground – Montgomery Waters Meadow Stadium

After 97 years at playing at Gay Meadow, the Shrews moved to a new stadium on the outskirts of the town. The *New Meadow* as it is known, is comprised of four separate stands which are functional and tidy, but lacks that certain something! The capacity is just under 10,000. In 2017 the stadium was renamed the Montgomery Waters Meadow Stadium as part of a corporate sponsorship deal. The Sky Blue Army were in the West Stand (pictured) for the 2019 match otherwise they were in the North Stand behind the goal.

It became the first stadium in England to introduce safe standing. Six rows of rail seats were installed at the rear of the South Stand. They can be switched from seating to standing.

Results
18 Sep 2012	1-4	League One	(Fleck)
31 Aug 2013	1-1	League One	(Wilson)
08 Mar 2016	1-2	League One	(Martin)
04 Mar 2017	0-0	League One	
22 Dec 2018	0-1	League One	
14 Dec 2019	1-2	League One	(Shipley)

The ground is around two miles out of town and a taxi ride from the station is recommended. Too many of our visits to Shrewsbury have been remembered for the problems with taxis. We have tried to get them to pick us up after the game from outside the ground or even from the pub down the road. Each time insisted they were at the pickup point as the game ended. The traffic around the ground is horrendous and we have had taxis arriving so late, being delayed on the way to the ground to pick us up, that we have missed our train back. On one occasion, not enough taxis were at the pickup point and we organised for those on the earlier trains to go first. I let Andy Knight who had a leg problem and had booked his travel independently, go in the first group of taxis only to miss my train as a result. Travelling back to Euston on my own, I was walking through the train as it approached Euston, only to pass Andy who was booked on the later train anyway.

It was 19 days short of 49 years since we last played at Shrewsbury when we played them in September 2012. Back in 1963 we had played at Gay Meadow, in the centre of town. The Shrews had moved to a new stadium on the outskirts of the town.

Pub

However, in 2012, with the match being played midweek there was no formal CCLSC trip arranged. I had booked a holiday cottage, just outside Shrewsbury for the week, so I could attend the Tranmere game on the previous Saturday and then the Tuesday evening game at Shrewsbury. We arranged to meet for the pre match drink at the CAMRA beer guide listed **Prince of Wales** on the Belle Vue estate. This is approximately 1.5 miles from the ground going towards the town centre. Shrewsbury Town memorabilia adorns the pub including some old seating from the old Gay Meadow ground.

Barry was there of course to meet up with me and others. He parked his car at the pub. It was a very long walk back afterwards, after the very depressing defeat that evening, which saw us in our lowest (then) league position for nearly half a century, Mark Robins was appointed a couple of days later.

As it was a new ground for many, and a Saturday, several more CCLSC members went in August 2013. The met at the **Three Fishes,** a 16th century building standing in the shadow of two churches, within the maze of streets and passageways in the medieval quarter of the town centre. The pub offered a range of real ales, including Stonehouse Station Bitter and the classic Timothy Taylor Landlord, and had an extensive food menu.

The ground is about three miles from the pub so it is was the CCLSC taxi service that was once again put into operation, although there is a bus service from the town centre to the ground. As our string of taxis arrived at the

Three Fishes, another small group of Cov fans tried, unsuccessfully, to hijack one of our cabs. Pre booking had paid dividends!

After the 1-1 draw, we entered September 2013 on minus two points and with Callum Wilson the League One's top scorer. Under the circumstances this was a tremendous achievement having started the season with a 10 point deduction.

Our next visit in March 2016, another evening game, those that had time went to the Three Fishes, in the town centre. Others went back to the Prince of Wales. A few, who had driven, went to the nearest pub to the ground, the Brooklands Hotel, just off the large island by the ground. It is about five minutes walk away from the stadium. It is a home fans only pub for certain high profile games.

In March 2017 we returned to the Three Fishes. The taxis were late but arrived eventually to take us out to the ground. This was the game that had 22 minutes of added time at the end of the first half following the head injury to Andy Rose.

The largest following of members went to the December 2018 game. It was clear that the Three Fishes was going to be too small and not able to accommodate our group this time. When needed to search for an alternative pub.

The **Coach & Horses,** set in a quiet street just off the High Street proved a great success. The pub is Victorian in style, with a wood-panelled bar, a small snug and a larger lounge/restaurant area. It has been a constant presence in the CAMRA Good Beer Guide for 20

years. It serves 3 regular beers, Salopian Oracle, Shropshire Gold and Stonehouse Station bitter, together with 3 changing beers, which often includes a Mild.

Being the last Saturday in December, we were informed that the Coach would only be offering their Christmas menu on our Saturday lunchtime visit. Emma reserved an area for those members who had pre ordered food. We were extremely well looked after by Emma and her team. The excellent beers and great food had the CCLSC members voting the Coach & Horses their 2018/19 Pub of the Season.

The quirk of the fixtures resulted in our next season's visit in 2019 also being in December. I was to present to Emma the belated CCLSC Pub of the Season Award in front of over 40 members, of which a large number enjoyed another Christmas meal. Emma was delighted to receive the award, especially when she was informed that whilst the quality of the real ale was important, we also considered the welcome we received, the atmosphere in the pub and the quality of the food in making our decision.

Despite the meticulous ordering of the food, I was to eat the wrong dessert and Ross Sauvage, couldn't make up his mind about whether or not he would want a dessert when we pre ordered. He did on the day, paid for his dessert separately, and when Treasurer Kev settled the bill for the group, we realised afterwards we had been charged for one more dessert. No one to this day is clear if we were charged for the extra dessert, eaten by me or they hadn't realised Ross had already paid. We never went back to Emma to check and our accounts that season show a small write off!

Southend United

Ground – Roots Hall

Roots Hall has four tall traditional floodlighting pylons. These are becoming rare as grounds are modernised. The capacity is 12,300 and there are flats overlooking the pitch above the South Stand. The Sky Blues Army were in the North Stand (pictured). It is a former terrace and the leg room and height distance between each row is less than desirable.

The closest station to the ground is Prittlewell, about a five minute walk away. Southend has two main stations. Southend Victoria is served by trains from London Liverpool Street, and Southend Central station with services from Fenchurch Street. Both have a journey time of around 1 hour from central London.

In January 2016 those joining us for pre match drinks were advised to stay on the train for one further stop past Prittlewell to Southend Victoria.

Pub

The **Olde Trout Tavern**. is within walking distance from the High Street and both mainline stations. It is a 15-20 walk to the ground. The pub name is said to derive from a term of endearment used for Landlady Chrissie. To everyone's surprise she opted for the name and refused to budge. Apparently the Old Trout was not for turning! (according to their website). The house beer, Trout Ale, from the local George's brewery at Wakering, and three guest ales were served together with Westerns Rosie's Pig on draught. Hot meals and snacks were available at lunchtime but, with the expected numbers attending, John the landlord suggested that any food was ordered early. Upon arriving there were a number of other Coventry fans already in the pub. Our group was split up with a number finding seating upstairs. The cafe style environment upstairs was not to everyone liking.

We are not sure why but the pub sign at the Olde Trout Tavern, had the fish wearing a sky blue sweater - probably to thank the number of Sky Blues supporters who frequented the establishment before the game. The 3-0 defeat saw the Shrimps have ex City player Gary Deegan sent off and Mowbray's experienced new signings, Peter Ramage and Steven Hunt, made their debuts. A good day out spoilt by the football.

We were to return later in 2016, in the December. The house beer, Brentwood's Trout Ale, was now from the local Essex brewery. Travel Secretary Simon worked his magic to get us to arrive slightly earlier than last season and we were able to all be seated in the downstairs bar area this time around. Simon, in the white shirt pictured with Colin. Another defeat and we were 21st in the table.

In October 2018 trains from both Liverpool Street and Fenchurch went to Southend Central, due to a bus replacement service. The Olde Trout was a slightly longer walk but arriving before noon again ensured we were all seated downstairs. The 2-1 win, with a last minute Jodi Jones goal had many members celebrating back at the Trout after the game.

By February 2020, we were "on our way", as the SBA was now singing regularly. In the swirling conditions, caused by Storm Dennis, with 72% possession in the first half and hitting the woodwork twice, confidence abounded. Members half time predictions that we were going to win this match comfortably were well founded. It was the subs Callum O'Hare and Max Biamou who scored in the second half to claim three points at a very windy Southend.

It had been a return to the Olde Trout as was becoming customary, but this time, some members were disappointed with the lack of beer choice on the day and so visited the Railway Hotel after the game rather than return to the Trout. It is unlikely we will be returning to Southend for some time with their relegation and our promotion.

Stevenage
Ground – Lamex Stadium

Lamex Stadium, but is still known to many fans at Broadhall Way, has a capacity of 7,300. The whole stadium is compact and has two impressive stands whilst one end in particular needs some work. There is a pleasant view into some woodland at the far end. The Sky Blues Army got to use the best stand in the ground, the South Stand, which is an all seated and covered stand behind one goal (pictured).

Results

26 Dec 2012	3-1	League One	(Wood, Baker, McGoldrick)
05 Oct 2013	1-0	League One	(Clarke)
02 Aug 2014	1-2	Friendly	(Tudgay)
21 Nov 2017	1-1	League Two	(McNulty)
21 Jul 2018	0-2	Friendly	

In our first visit to Stevenage on Boxing Day 2012 everyone went home happy. Carl Baker scored to give Coventry the lead in the final minute of normal time and then David McGoldrick added a third in added time with a delightful lob from outside the box.

Pub

Our first ever league game at Stevenage was on Boxing Day 2012. A large number of CCLSC members were at the **Our Mutual Friend,** a 15 minute walk from the ground, before the game. This pub had been listed in every CAMRA Guide since 2002 and served an ever-changing selection of real ales. Unfortunately, the real ales on sale that day was served in plastic glasses - on police orders according to the bar staff - due to the large number of Coventry fans expected that day! Those members who returned to the pub after the match were rewarded with beer served in glass pints.

We met for our pre match drink in October 2013, at the **Marquis of Lorne,** in the centre of Stevenage. The Marquis came highly recommended by CCLSC member Jim Mcilwaine. It was the preferred choice to the Our Mutual Friend used the previous Boxing Day, as unfortunately, due to the

large number of Coventry fans expected again, we were anticipating beer would again be served in plastic glasses before the game at Our Mutual Friend. In contrast Mick Power, from the Marquis, ran an away fans friendly pub serving Greene King and guest real ales. Food and snacks were served throughout the day.

With the Marquis over a one mile away from the ground, we pre ordered taxis. The last taxi to arrive caused some confusion. The driver stopped opposite on a zebra crossing and as I and the last group went to get in the taxi a police car arrived. We thought he would just be moved on but the taxi driver became very animated with the police and it was clear the discussions were going to take some time. We never found out what happened but we had to order another taxi.

We played a pre season friendly at Stevenage in August 2014. We went to the **Chequers**. a Greene King pub with 5 regular guest beers. It was again recommended by Jim McIlwaine, who worked locally and was a regular at the Chequers.

We presented the 2013/14 CCLSC Player of the Season award before the Stevenage friendly. The traditional end of season award presentation hadn't taken place in 2014. With some members boycotting home games played at Sixfields, CCLSC decided to delay the presentation of the award and make it at an away game in the following pre season. Manager, Steve Pressley, accepted the award on behalf of Coventry City, from member Kev Monks. The award was to have been presented to the winner Joe Murphy, who by then had left for Huddersfield Town. Later that season Barry and Phil Smith took a detour to the Huddersfield training ground, on the way to Barnsley, to drop off the trophy to Joe Murphy.

I must mention a big, BIG, thank you to Clive Abrey and Stevenage FC for all their help in facilitating that day. They provided a car parking space for Barry, who was concerned about travelling with the trophy by train and taxi, an executive box for the nine members in the presentation party to meet, and

to be able to make the presentation at the front of the main stand. Even the Stevenage mascot wanted to get in on the act and they had even baked cup cakes for us with the Coventry City crest on them. I quoted Chris Webb in the newsletter, saying he hoped that we got drawn against Stevenage in the FA Cup so we can fill their away end as a thank you for their excellent hospitality.

It was an evening game in November 2017. CCLSC members returned to the Chequers. It served up to 8 real ales including the Greene King range. Food was served from 6pm. This game will be remembered more for the long term injury to Jodi Jones, who was stretchered off, than the disappointment about the performance that night.

Sara Robb, pictured below, was at the game. She was the membership secretary for many years, but due to her work commitments in TV Sport hasn't been a regular traveller in recent seasons. Whenever she can get to a game she joins us. Sara perhaps put it into context when she tweeted "not the worst performance of the season, England still holds that honour." Sara is a regular England supporter and has not missed a non tournament 'away' trip since 2003.

For the friendly in July 2018 we returned and were made welcome once again at the Chequers.

Sunderland
Ground - Stadium of Light

A large stadium holding 49,000 is totally enclosed. However half the stadium is higher than the other giving it a somewhat unbalanced feel. The Sky Blue Army were in Upper Tier of North Stand at one end of the ground (pictured in the distance). You do have to climb a large number of flights of stairs to reach the top tier.

Results
13 Apr 2019   5-4   League One   (Enobakhare, Bakayoko, Hiwala, Shipley, Chaplin)
23 Nov 2019   1-1   League One   (Hyam)

Pub

With their double relegation this big club, found themselves in League One. We were to play them at the Stadium of Light twice in 2019.

In April, it was trains, planes and motor cars to get to Sunderland. Several members travelled up and stayed for the weekend. It didn't help those starting their journey north early that day that the Metro between Newcastle and Sunderland wasn't in service.

It did allow a drink or two at the **Centurion** at Newcastle station before boarding the extremely overcrowded train to Sunderland. It was originally built as a First Class lounge and the large one room pub served a variety of cask ales, including Black Sheep Best Bitter and Caledonian Deuchars IPA.

A few members, like Alastair Laurie, tried the metro bus replacement service but in doing so missed the scheduled train on the return to London.

We were welcomed at the **Dun Cow**, in central Sunderland. It served beers on up to 7 handpumps. It offered CAMRA members 10% discount on real ales. The Grade II listed building features in the CAMRA National Inventory. General Manager Daniel advised that Amore Italia use their kitchen space and he could not guarantee food availability, for the numbers of our members likely to attend, unless they used the restaurant space upstairs. However, they did have a sister venue the Firestation, in the next street, who had much more seating and a large food menu. It also has a good selection of beers and offered CAMRA discount. The overcrowding was not just on the trains, as the small rooms usually occupied by Sunderland fans, were taken over at the Dun Cow.

'Memorable' can take many forms. The game at the Stadium of Light was an example. It was a dream for statisticians and record keepers. It may have been 5-4 but 2 of the Sunderland goals were deflected and a third was a complete clanger from keeper Lee Burge. The quality of our goals, and our ability to counter-attack were unbelievable. One of the games that will be remembered for years to come for those that could say "I was there".

The Sky Blue Army were in the Upper Tier of North Stand and those sitting towards the back had a good view of the pitch but had a limited view of the rest of the stadium. That didn't stop the songs about seeing the Sunderland fans crying on the Telly. The 5-4 win was to feature in the Netflix series, Sunderland 'Til I Die.

In November 2019, there was major Network Rail engineering works planned for the weekend on the route north. Trains would take 4 and a half hours up and 6 hours on the return journey. No advance train tickets were available and the cost of travel was just exorbitant. I found I could fly from Gatwick via Dublin to Newcastle cheaper than the cost of the rail fare. Unfortunately, the return journey by air wasn't possible that evening. Those few members who managed to get to Sunderland that day joined me at the Centurion on Newcastle station for their pre match drinks. Once again, the Metro wasn't working that day. The Newcastle to Sunderland train was once again extremely overcrowded.

To catch the last train back to London meant catching the 5.25pm from Sunderland. This arrived into Newcastle 5 minutes before the last scheduled London train that day left. This hourly service, with no Metro, was like the Japanese underground with staff pushing customers on to the train. The

Newcastle bound train finally left about 10 minutes late. I was pushed up against a door chatting to a Dad and his son, Sunderland supporters, who wanted to get off at the only stop between Sunderland and Newcastle. The train stopped at their station but the doors would not open. After a few more minutes trying to open the doors the train left without letting any of the passengers off.

I arrived into Newcastle after my London service had left. Speaking to the train staff they said that a train was due in shortly from Edinburgh, and would be stopping at Newcastle. This had not been on the timetable. The train manager allowed me on, despite an advanced ticket on the previous train. He was aware of the train disruptions around Newcastle that day. The train stopped at Darlington and a few minutes later, Tim Fisher walked past on his way to the buffet. I joined Tim and his partner for the journey back to London. He had been driven from Sunderland to Darlington, where he was aware that a later train back to London stopped and thereby missed the Sunderland to Newcastle train disruption. If we do play Sunderland again, perhaps going via Darlington will be worth looking into.

Barry pictured with Paul and Beverley Clay at the Dun Cow.

Sutton United
Ground – Gander Green Lane

Copyright Paul Willott

The ground holds 5,000 and was very different to that experienced at our infamous FA Cup defeat in 1989. Both ends now had small covered terraces, which are both similar in design. Sutton installed an artificial 3G playing surface in 2015.

Results
08 Jul 2017	1-0	Friendly	(Moorhouse)
07 Jul 2018	0-2	Friendly	

Pub

We were to play two pre-season friendlies at Gander Green Lane in 2017 and 2018. These were part of the deal when signing Max Biamou. For some members this was the only non league ground they knew the name of, and was very different to that many of those CCLSC members attending at the infamous FA Cup defeat in 1989 had remembered.

For the July 2017 game we had tables booked at the **Cock & Bull**, in Sutton High Street, a short walk from the Sutton station. This was a Fullers Ale House and served three Fuller beers with a 15% CAMRA discount. The building is a former bank branch, converted into a spacious one bar pub. Members pictured below, jumped back on the train at Sutton for the 3 minute journey to West Sutton, which is next to the ground.

The following July, in 2018, the kick off was bought forward to a 1pm kick off, due to England playing later that afternoon. As a result, members met at the **Moon on the Hill**, a Wetherspoon pub, from around 11.00 pm. The Cock & Bull didn't open until noon.

Many members stayed behind in the Sutton Clubhouse to watch the England Quarter Final game on their large screens. Barry and I had arranged to meet up with Chief Executive Dave Boddy after the game to discuss with him our concerns about how we could continue to obtain away match tickets for CCLSC members going forward. The Club had announced that they would not be providing away season tickets for the coming season (due to constraints with the ticketing administrator). Dave listened to our concerns and arranged for the Ticket office to provide tickets together for our members for away games. Barry presented Shelagh, pictured, from the ticket office with flowers and chocolates as a thank you for all her help with CCLSC ticket requests.

Several members will remember that Tim Fisher joined us on the bus back to Sutton station after the game. A Chairman on public transport with supporters talking about the coming season's expectations is not seen everywhere.

Swindon Town
Ground –Energy Check County Ground

Those members who had visited during Swindon's car-crash of a season in the Premiership in 1993-94 did not notice much of a change to the ground on our non Championship visits. The open terrace at one end now had seats, plus some general deterioration. With the exception of the attractive Don Rogers Stand, opposite the away fans, the ground has a tired look.

The Sky Blue Army were in the Arkell Stand (pictured). This is an old stand with facilities to match. Both exits from the stand went into the same concourse area. This had one window to a kiosk at one end, the toilets at the other and a staircase leading down in the middle. Before, and especially at halftime and at the end of the game this area became a bottleneck and very crowded. On some occasions we also had supporters in the open terrace behind the goal.

Results

13 Oct 2012	2-2	League One	(McGoldrick 2)
21 Dec 2013	1-2	League One	(Clarke)
30 Aug 2014	1-1	League One	(McQuoid)
24 Oct 2015	2-2	League One	(Vincelot, Tudgay)
06 Aug 2016	0-1	League One	
26 Sep 2017	2-1	League One	(Doyle, Nazon)
27 Jul 2019	2-0	Friendly	(Bakayoko, Biamou)

Pub

Swindon has become one of the most talked about trips over the years. We regularly visited the **Glue Pot** near the station, which served Hop Back and Downton ales but it did not serve hot food at the weekends, only filled rolls. Situated in the centre of Brunel's Railway Village, the Gluepot's corner shop appearance belies the drinking treasures to be found within. The pub gets its name from the railway coachbuilders who would bring their gluepots with them when they took their breaks. The Gluepot is unashamedly a real old-fashioned pub with old-fashioned values.

On the visit in October 2012 everyone had heard the story from a previous visit of Ross asking for a lager and the barman, to everyone's amusement, looking around the bar and under the bar before proclaiming they didn't serve lager.

The following season in December 2013 our visit was to become CCLSC folklore. The Glue Pot had been contacted the week before and our pub and directions email sent out saying we were being welcomed back. On the Friday evening whilst out with Chris my wife, my Blackberry (remember those) was going mad. Trying desperately to ignore it I eventually read the various messages saying that one member had contacted the pub about food and was told it wasn't opening.

I subsequently spoke to the landlord late that evening who informed me that the Police Football Intelligence Officer had contacted him about internet traffic which suggested that a planned fight was to take place at the Glue Pot before the game. As such he was being requested not to open before 3pm. He was very apologetic as he had welcomed CCLSC members the previous year and was looking forward to welcoming us back.

We urgently made arrangements to meet at the **Great Western,** also known as the **GW**, a Victorian railway hotel opposite the railway station. Two Arkell's regular beers plus a seasonal one were on

offer. It is one of the West Midlands Police designated away fans pubs, so not a pub we regularly would have visited.

What an eventful day it was to become. We were met at the station by a large police presence and directed across the road to the GW. We were made especially welcome by the landlord despite him not being aware we were coming. When his chef didn't turn up, meaning no food was available, he did provide sandwiches, bowls of chips and sausages free of charge to the 30 members, including two members Gary Hickman from Germany and Michael Sykes from New Zealand, presumably as a thank you for drinking him dry of Wiltshire Gold the excellent local ale.

As it approached 2:30, those members still in the pub were then escorted to the ground. It was like being back in the 70s I heard one member comment.

Charles regularly tells the story that he asked a copper what this was all about and he said "we expected you would be younger". The average age of those being escorted was nearer 50. This farcical show of police strength included three horses, two police vans and nearly as many police officers as fans.

Traffic was stopped at junctions to allow us to cross roads and in speaking to several of the police officers they seemed to confirm that they had picked up considerable internet traffic that there was to be an attack on Cov fans who were meeting at the Glue Pot. Was this as a result of the pub and directions

email sent out to members? The pub itself was not one of the designated away fans pubs and is somewhat out of the way. Joking apart, we did discuss whether we needed to use code when sending out the details of the pubs we planned to visit in future.

The police presence after the game further confounded the best of us. Having escorted us to the ground, we along with all the other Sky Blues fans were then faced with a large line of police stopping fans from going the way they had come to ground. We were directed to walk around the ground, across a very muddy field, onto a darkened road none of us had been on before. There was little police presence at this point or directions of how to get back to the station. How this was to "protect" visiting fans, as one police officer said, was totally baffling.

We were to return in August 2014 to the GW. Gavin, the Manager, informed me that he had already made a note of the date of Coventry's visit and had hoped that we would be returning again that season to the GW. "Look out for the designated CCLSC seating area to the left of the bar as you enter the GW" he told us. We were provided with a free curry by the pub as a thank you for returning. Group pictured below.

In October 2015 we were to return to the Glue Pot. Simon Fahy, who had been working on a project requiring him to be in Swindon on several occasions, had seen that the GW had been prosecuted for food poisoning. We also had successful visits in August 2016 and September 2017 to the Glue Pot.

SBI members Steve Pittam, from Dubai, pictured far right, and Robert Gauci, (left) from Malta, joined us at Swindon in August 2016. They are pictured below with Phil Smith, who was an original SBI member, when based overseas.

We did plan a return to the Glue Pot for the 2019 pre season friendly. Many members had fond memories of the Glue Pot and were looking forward to a return visit. We were met at the door with the sign "sorry, closed due to toilet leak awaiting plumber". We moved on to the Wyvern Tavern in the town centre. The WhatsApp was going full throttle as members arriving into Swindon were directed to the Wyvern Tavern.

Tottenham Hotspur
Ground – White Hart Lane

Once you get inside the hulking mass of concrete that was White Hart Lane, a whole new world opened up - totally enclosed and two-tiered, it was well balanced. In many ways it was one of the best grounds in the country. A genuine football ground, not an 'arena', and had real character to it, so it's a shame it isn't more widely praised. The (relative) lack of capacity, back then set at 38,000, meant that the club was back then thinking of relocating, which would see the loss of a really special English football ground. Away fans normally had both tiers of one of the corners but with our larger allocation for the FA Cup match the Sky Blue Army had an extended area in the South Stand. The legroom, facilities, access etc were as good as you would expect for a Premier League ground. White Hart Lane was a great place to watch football and one of the last remaining large genuine football grounds, with a certain beauty to its sweeping design.

Results
05 Jan 2013   0-3   FA Cup

Pub

We were drawn against Spurs in the FA Cup in January 2013. We had over 5,000 of the SBA attend, along with a very large CCLSC following.

As many members had not visited White Hart Lane for many years and the pubs visited pre relegation had been the Two Brewers on Scotland Green, which was looted by rioters in the Tottenham riots in August 2011 and was by then designated as a home fans pub, and the Antwerp Arms, which was closed in 2011 following a fire but had recently re-opened. A lot of pubs in the area of the ground were home-centric and a little uncompromising, so we decided to meet up for a pre match drink near Liverpool Street station, in Central London. The recommended pub, The Magpie, we found out on the Friday didn't open on a Saturday despite what their website stated. I subsequently discovered my email had been answered by head office rather than the pub itself. Charles Tomkins, who at that time worked near Liverpool Street, was passing on the Friday and noticed the pub sign stating it was closed over the weekend.

We therefore met at The **Lord Aberconway** which is a short stroll from Liverpool Street station. This historical Nicholson pub did hearty pub meals at decent prices and had a range of real ales. It is supposedly haunted, and some say the spirits responsible are victims of the Great Fire of London.

Not everyone had smartphones back then, and in the rush to get messages out to members on the Friday evening about the change of pub, I completely forgot to call the Lord Aberconway beforehand. If I had done so, I probably would have advised them to expect around 25 and not the 75-100 who popped in. As such, the manager was the only person serving, expecting his usual half a dozen or so Saturday lunchtime customers, and not the large number of CCLSC fans. I am sure the manager did not need to go on any January diet given the perspiring he did that day! CCSLC finished off all four real ale barrels that lunchtime, much to his delight I suspect. Any delay in getting served didn't detract from the atmosphere in this classic old London pub. Food was stopped being served about 15 minutes after opening, as the cook couldn't cope and became the glass collector to keep the beers flowing.

Lambo proudly unveiled his Wembley 1987 flag at the Lord Aberconway.

Upon leaving the pub, the train journey out to White Hart Lane was reminiscent of the train journey to Villa Park on that fateful date we were relegated from the Premier League. It was jammed with everyone singing the Sky Blue song. Upon returning to Liverpool Street after the game, a few members thought about a final pint back at the Lord Aberconway. We were to be disappointed. There was a large sign on the door which stated it was closed that Saturday evening, 'as it had run out of beer'.

Tranmere Rovers
Ground – Prenton Park

Prenton Park is fairly modern and all seated with a capacity of 16,500. The ground is dominated by the Kop Stand at one end of the stadium which has a capacity of around 5,500 and dwarfs the rest of the ground. It replaced a former open terrace.

The Sky Blue Army were in the affectionately named Cowshed stand at one end of the ground (pictured). It offers a good view in a stand that is much larger at one end than the other, sloping downwards towards one side. This reminded older members of the stand at the old Dell at Southampton.

Results
15 Sep 2012   0-2   **League One**
22 Feb 2014   1-3   **League One**   **(Petrasso)**
01 Jan 2020   4-1   **League One**   **(Godden 3, Shipley)**

Pub

One of our early away fixtures in September 2012 the CCLSC train travellers arrived into Birkenhead at 11am so went to the nearby Wetherspoon pub for their all-day breakfast, which suited Colin Henderson who had left the South Coast at 5.30 am that morning.

I had travelled from Shrewsbury that day, via Chester, from our rented holiday cottage (we were playing Shrewsbury the following Tuesday).

On that sunny afternoon our group of over 30 members sat in the garden at **Gallaghers Pub and Barbers Shop,** a 10-15 minute walk from Birkenhead Central, but unfortunately away from the ground. It is close to the famous Mersey Ferries and was CAMRA Wirral Pub of the Year for 2011, so it was worth the walk. Those travelling from Liverpool Lime Street alighted at Birkenhead Hamilton Square (one stop before Birkenhead Central).

Upon arrival at Gallaghers, which opened at noon, we discovered that the landlord, chef and most of the staff had gone to a CAMRA beer festival so no food was available. The Wetherspoons' breakfast and the hot pies bought in from the local fish & chip shop supplemented the local ales or Pinot Grigio, in the case of Mark Smith (front left) and Jonathan Strange (front right). The fully functional barber shop meant men could take advantage of one of their hot

towel shaves, leaving them fully invigorated. No one took up the challenge!

Prenton Park is a 30 minute walk away and so it was taxis from the pub. There is a taxi rank outside Hamilton Square station, just around the corner.

For our next visit, in February 2014, owners, Kevin and Sue Gallagher, who have won numerous CAMRA awards over the years, were there this time to welcome us. We had travelled via Chester rather than go into Liverpool Lime Street this time for cost reasons. Therefore after the game we walked back to Rock Ferry station, 15 minutes from the ground. The first group, having left quickly after our 3-1 defeat, found a pub near Rock Ferry station. It didn't serve any real ale, the carpets were swimming in something not that nice and they were offered meat packs amongst other local delights. Those arriving slightly later, like myself, refused to have a drink.

New Year's Day 2020 meant only a small group of 10 travelled but we still met at Gallaghers. The game will be remembered for Matty Godden scoring his second hat trick in a few days, and for the atrocious pitch. Honestly, the Sunday League pitch in my Kent village was in better condition that January than the mud bath of a pitch at Prenton Park.

The barber's shop business had closed in October 2016 creating a much larger room. There was also a retractable roof fitted to the outside area. It served up to 5 changing beers. Unfortunately, Frank and Sue had informed me that their kitchen would be closed on New Year's Day but we could bring in our own food to consume in the pub.

Adrian and Stuart, pictured, who would regularly join us for northern games were at the Gallagher.

Taxis were pre booked after the game, as we needed to get back to Birkenhead Central quickly. There was only one connection that got us back to Liverpool Lime Street in time for our trains south. Traffic meant that the driver recommended he took us straight to Lime Street. We thought a Scouse tactic was being played but the taxi driver got us back at Lime Street in good time for us to get a drink and food, before boarding our train back to London.

Walsall
Ground – Banks's Stadium (still known as the Bescot Stadium)

The warehouse-esque Bescot Stadium, with its capacity of 11,300 is probably my least favourite ground. The next time our members moan about the Ricoh, they should take a moment to imagine having to watch home games from behind pillars in this gloomy and cramped ground. It does have a large stand at one end which differentiates it from similar stadiums like Scunthorpe's Glenford Park.

The Sky Blue Army were in the stand at the other end of the ground. There are a number of supporting pillars at the front which impedes your view. In addition, Walsall season-ticket holders in the Family Stand, along the side of the pitch, were moved for several of the Coventry games so that the whole of this stand could be allocated to Sky Blue supporters.

Results

Date	Score	Competition	Scorers
01 Apr 2013	0-4	League One	
26 Oct 2013	1-0	League One	(Moussa)
03 Jan 2015	2-0	League One	(O'Brien, Tudgay)
22 Aug 2015	1-2	League One	(Murphy)
29 Oct 2016	1-1	League One	(Rose)
03 Oct 2017	2-2	FL Trophy	(McNulty, Ponticelli)
10 Nov 2018	2-3	FA Cup	(Clarke-Harris, Thomas)
08 Dec 2018	1-2	League One	(Thomas)

Pub

We were to play Walsall several times during this period. The ground has its own railway station, Bescot Stadium, situated behind the away end. It is on the opposite side of the delightful M6 flyover.

The annual chaos getting away from the Bescot station, after the Walsall game, meant that on several occasions our group was split up with some only just catching the 18.30 from Birmingham New Street back to Euston. It is not that they didn't know in advance that there would be several thousand away fans that day!

For the Easter Monday 2013 derby game there were a limited choice of pubs in and around the ground and the idea of drinking in the centre of Birmingham at the Wellington was discounted with Birmingham City playing at home to Wolves on the same day.

 So CCLSC members went to the **Black Country Arms**, near the Walsall railway station (NOT Bescot Stadium station nearest to the ground). A sister pub to the *Wellington* in Birmingham, it is located just off the market in the town centre. The pub is multi - levelled and has masses of polished wood and Victorian high ceilings. Whilst it has various quieter areas we would gather in the larger upstairs area. It serves good food and boasts over 10 hand pumps. The pub has been a local CAMRA Pub of the Year on several occasions.

Members joining us were asked to stay on the train from Birmingham New Street for one additional stop after Bescot Stadium station. We did receive some funny looks from other Sky Blues supporters who were alighting at Bescot. The group would return from Walsall just before kickoff. This was to work successfully on all our visits.

Honorary members Rod Dean (left) and Jim Brown pictured at the Easter game. Lambo, however drove to the Easter Sunday game, and parking outside the pub received a parking ticket for his troubles. Rob Parker thought he would leave his car in Walsall, as catching the train going towards Walsall, rather than Birmingham with thousands of Sky Blues fans, would speed his getaway. It proved not to be so. The police wouldn't let him through the crowds queuing under the motorway, to go over the railway bridge to the Walsall direction platform.

It was a return to the Black Country Arms (BCA), in October 2013, before the Walsall game. Upon arrival we discovered, that in addition to their usual extensive range of real ale, they had a Welsh beer festival that weekend, adding several more excellent beers.

We were to return in January 2015, August 2015, October 2016 and October 2017. We returned twice in 2018, in November, for an FA Cup tie, and December.

Our travel secretary would ensure that we arrived into Walsall just before noon so our group arrived before opening time to ensure we reserved the upstairs balcony area.

Standing outside on one occasion, patiently waiting for the doors to be opened, we were chatting with a BCA regular. When the doors opened he said to the young barman that he had a few more customers than normal that day. The youngster said begrudgingly that was why he had been dragged in so early.

Pictured below are Mick and Tom Furnival-Adams at the BCA.

The BCA were celebrating their 10th anniversary and had another beer festival on at the pub before the FA Cup tie in December 2018.

Watford
Ground – Vicarage Road

Vicarage Road had been significantly improved since our Premier and Championship visits when we played them in 2019. The Sir Elton John Stand was now open, instead of the building site we had seen previously. The capacity is now 21,500. The Sky Blue Army were in the Vicarage Road stand (pictured) for the League Cup game.

Results
30 Jul 2014   1-0   Friendly   (Tudgay)
27 Aug 2019   0-3   League Cup

Pub

In July 2014 when we played a pre season friendly against Watford, it was played not at Vicarage Road but at a very smart Boreham Wood ground. Given the easy of journey from St Pancras we had a dozen or so CCLSC members attending. We met at the Wetherspoon pub **Hart & Spool** near the ground

A group of members pictured at the Hart & Spool on a hot July evening.

The Coventry Telegraph pictured our group in the ground.

We were to meet Watford, then in the Premier League, in the League Cup in August 2019. Most members arrived at Watford Junction, so we met at the **Wellington Arms**, some 300m away. The pub is about a 20 minute walk from the ground.

This modernised street corner pub served Fuller's London Pride and Tring guest Ales. Warren, the manager, informed me that food was available and there was also a decent chippie across the road, whose food is allowed into the Wellington.

The beer selection and food choice could have been better and several members recalled previous visits, back in the Championship years, to the Estcourt Arms. This was another example of our policy of choosing pubs close to the station or ground for evening fixtures not being ideal but practical.

We were finally outclassed and went down to a 3-0 defeat, and our mood wasn't helped with all the fast trains back into London from Watford that evening cancelled resulting in the slow trains taking the equivalent time as our usual Coventry to Euston journey time.

Phil Higgins pictured at the ground.

Wembley
Ground Wembley Stadium

For both Finals the very large Sky Blue Army were in the West Stand with the majority of CCLSC members who obtained tickets through us, located in Block 133 behind the goal.

Results
02 Apr 2017   2-1   Checkatrade Final
(Bigirimana, Thomas)
28 May 2018 3-1   League Two Play-off Final
(Willis, Shipley, Grimmer)

We were to play Oxford United in the Checkatrade Trophy Final on Sunday 2 April 2017. It had been thirty years since our last appearance at Wembley and the first at the new stadium. It was a privilege to be at Wembley that day. Never let anyone tell you that football doesn't matter. Well done to all the SBA. I, like many, felt proud to be a Sky Blues supporter that day.

CCLSC members from London, the South East and beyond were out in force. They had travelled from around the globe, left home early to get their planes, trains or cars into London more in hope than expectation. Win, lose or draw they probably didn't really care, as long as there was passion from the players to match that of the SBA. And didn't they do just that.

International based members were there from the US, Canada, the Middle East as well as most European countries. As always, the Scandinavian countries were well represented. Danes, Norwegians, Swedes and Finns were all there.

Sky Blue support of over 43,000 was at Wembley, with thousands more watching on TV throughout the country and around the world. It was to be a day to show the potential of our team and club, and celebrate everything Sky Blue.

 With the kick off at 2.30pm and many members wanting to take in the Wembley atmosphere we met very early at the **Calthorpe Arms**, a few minutes' walk from Kings Cross/St Pancras station in central London.

With a journey time from the Calthorpe to your Wembley seat of about an hour, Adrian, the landlord, and a long standing CCLSC member, opened the pub at 10.30 am and served up food that Sunday morning. A simplified menu was available on a pre ordered only basis. When I arrived just before 10.30 am there was already a large queue outside waiting for the pub to open. I am not sure why but for some reason the Young's beers tasted even better than normal that day.

The BBC Coventry & Warwickshire Radio CWR sent reporter Marian McNamee to join us at the Calthorpe Arms. She conducted live radio interviews that morning with members, including myself and several SBI Members from Norway, Russia, Germany and the USA. She joined me and several other members on the tube out to Wembley and continued her interviews down Olympic Way, speaking to member Rod Williams.

Martin Wesson based in Germany shown being interviewed outside the Calthorpe Arms

I deputised, in this instance for Barry, in distributing the match tickets that Sunday. Jorg Nannestad coordinated a group of 26 Norwegian based supporters, and along with members from Germany, Russia and the US all collected their match tickets from me at the Calthorpe Arms that morning. Pictured here is me handing over the Norwegian match tickets to Jorg.

Pictured below is a packed Calthorpe Arms early on that Sunday morning.

It was not possible for everyone to get into central London and the Calthorpe before the game.

Barry had done a fantastic job with liaising with the Ticket Office to arrange for over 200 of our members to be seated together. He and several of his family members arranged to stay overnight at the Holiday Inn, near Wembley, and as such he wasn't able to meet up with the rest of us at the Calthorpe Arms, having his pre match drinks at the hotel bar.

My wife, Chris, son in law Sean, heavily pregnant daughter, Nikki, didn't feel they could travel from Kent early to join my son Mark and I at the Calthorpe. They travelled directly to Wembley and we planned to meet up at the Green Man. Chris recalls the Green Man as the pub with two cubicles of flooded delight having queued up for warm lager in plastic glasses. I have to say that I have seen other accounts from Sky Blues supporters saying what a fantastic atmosphere there was at the Green Man that day. This was perhaps yet another example of why CCLSC meet at real ale pubs away from the ground.

It is not only international based supporters who were coming from far and wide. I should mention two of our CCLSC committee members and their travels to get to Wembley that day.

Our Chair, Colin Henderson arrived into Gatwick from Florida on the morning of the final. He had only travelled out to the USA on Thursday, but left his wife Rachael in the sunshine to make a fleeting visit back to the UK for the game. He returned to Florida on the Monday to continue his holiday.

Robin Ogleby was in Madrid and curtailed a friend's 50th birthday weekend to arrive back on Sunday morning in time for the final. Apparently, Sue his wife, wasn't that enthusiastic about their 7 am flight home.

Their exploits were perhaps surpassed by Helsinki based Hannu Solanne, who over the years has been over to see the Sky Blues on two or three occasions a season. He was visiting his daughter who lives in Australia at the time. How could he not be at Wembley? He flew back to Helsinki, then onto London for the final before returning back to Helsinki. He then flew back out to continue his visit to his daughter in Australia. That is some commitment.

As Hannu said, "how could he not be at Wembley that day? It was an easy decision to make."

It was about memories that today. Seeing 43,000 Sky Blues supporters enjoying their day and, as we now know - bringing home a trophy.

Memories are made of this. Here is an extract I wrote in the CCLSC May 2017 Newsletter -

"The Wembley memories

Back in 1987, there was a "Seven" in the year, Coventry City get to a Wembley final. The Sky Blues are underdogs.

In the second half, playing towards the large SBA, the ball is played out to the wing. Dave Bennett (Benno) sends over a superb cross for Keith Houchen to score the goal of the game, if not the season.

Captain Brian Kilcline goes off injured but returns to collect the cup.

Fast forward to 2017, there is a "Seven" in the year, Coventry City get to a Wembley final. The Sky Blues are underdogs.

In the second half, playing towards the large SBA, the ball is played out to the wing. Kyel Reid (Reido) sends over a superb cross for George Thomas to score the goal of the game, if not the season.

Captain Jordan Willis goes off injured but returns to collect the cup.

Was it meant to be?"

Just like the buses in Broadgate, when I was growing up in Coventry, or so the saying went, you wait for ages and then they all come along together. After a thirty year wait, we have a Cup win in 2017, and we were back at Wembley in May 2018.

The Play-Off Final against Exeter was on Monday 28 May 2018.

It was to be a double promotion for the City of Coventry. The "real" Cov Rugby Club also won promotion that season. Promotion at the first time of asking was achieved by the Sky Blues on a hot sunny day to remember at Wembley. The Sky was certainly Sky Blue.

It was pandemonium! The noise, the atmosphere, and the celebrations. Over 37,000 Sky Blues supporters returned to Wembley for the second time in just over 12 months.

Jordan Willis showed the first touch of a top class striker before curling the ball in the far corner for first goal. Man of the Match Marc McNulty, tormented Exeter all afternoon, and he held the ball up long enough before making the perfect lay off pass for Jordon Shipley to hit it first time, getting a deflection before it nestled in the net. Jack Grimmer, who gained national recognition for his FA Cup goal against Stoke earlier in the season, scored arguably the best of the goals with a delightful left footed unstoppable shot to send the SBA into raptures. A late Exeter goal didn't take way the party atmosphere.

On the evening we had won 4–1 at Notts County in the semi-final, we received the announcement that Wembley tickets were going on sale the following morning. So we were not able to liaise with the Ticket Office this time around. Operation-get-tickets went into full swing. We asked CCLSC members who were season ticket holders to purchase the maximum six tickets they were allowed. We asked them to get tickets in the same block at Wembley. A Wembley ticketing team was established and I joined Barry, Rob, Charles, and especially Matt Chattaway, with ticket allocation and distribution. This eventually went well, but not after long hours of hard effort.

 With several people therefore obtaining tickets for other CCLSC members, timing meant it was not possible to post tickets to members in this instance. We had to insist that if members had tickets for other members or needed to collect tickets themselves they needed to be collected on the day of the game at the designated pub, the **Feathers**. The Feathers is opposite St James's Park tube station (on the Central and District line) and about 900m from Victoria station. It features the motif of the Prince of Wale's ostrich feathers in this imposing Flemish style red brick 1898 pub, which was designed for the (then) New Westminster Brewery.

Barry was in his element at the Feathers as he distributed 150 plus tickets to members on the morning of the Final.

Sophie, the Manager, opened the pub at 10.30 am on Bank Holiday Monday and served up to eight real ales. As food was not available until noon, and recognising that some of our members may wish to leave early for Wembley, Sophie allowed food from the nearby sandwich outlets to be bought into the pub. Robin Ogleby reported back how pleased Sophie was with beer sales and the sheer amount of people who turned up.

Of course, for those who couldn't get to Wembley there were gatherings around the world. SBI Members gathered to watch the game in places like Oslo (pictured below), Hong Kong and California, with other individuals watching from home. It was not a holiday in the Cayman Islands so Mark White took a half days holiday so he could watch the game

West Bromwich Albion
Ground – The Hawthorns

The Hawthorns is a compact ground with a capacity of 27,000. It has a mixture of different looking stands. The Sky Blues Army were in the Smethwick End (pictured) It has its own Railway and Metro Station about a five minute walk from the Hawthorns ground. One slightly annoying feature was that the large metal gate at the back of the Smethwick End, which was open before the game, was closed after. This resulted in those wanting to get back to the station having to walk through the back streets adding considerable time to the journey.

Results
28 July 2018   2-5   Friendly   (Allassani, Thompson)

Pub

We met at the **Wellington** for the Cyrille Regis Memorial Trophy game in July 2018. There was a larger than expected CCLSC contingent at the pre season friendly who met near Birmingham New Street station.

Wigan Athletic
Ground – DW Stadium

The DW Stadium holds 25,000 and has four separate stands of roughly the same height. The stadium is shared with Wigan Warriors Rugby League team.

For a new designed stadium the concourse and toilets did not seem to be able to cope with our large away following. The Sky Blue Army were in the North Stand. The photo is taken from the away end.

Our tickets were at the back and high up the steep steps in the stand. Eric Whiting and Phil Smith asked if they could swap their seats to be near the exit and lower down the stand. We did have some unpleasant experiences with over officious stewards that day trying to get people in their correct seats. This was opposite from some grounds where they operated a sit anywhere policy.

Results
09 April 2016   **0-1**   **League One**

In April 2016 CCLSC members met at the **Raven Hotel**. This Grade II listed building is a superb example of a 1900's Commercial Hotel. Upon arrival at this town centre pub there was some concern about how very crowded it looked as we entered. However, contacting them beforehand ensured we had a designated area set aside at the back of the pub.

The Raven had five handpumps serving real ale from mainly local breweries on a rotating basis. The Raven Ale, from Blonde Witches Moorhouse brewery, complemented their pies perfectly. It served classic pub food, basket meals as well as their specialty home-made pies. Apparently, it had the only singing chef in Wigan! From the Wigan North Western railway station it was a short (3 minute) walk up Wallgate. It was a 25-30 minute walk to the ground.

Wolverhampton Wanderers
Ground -Molineux

An impressive ground (for League One) holding 32,000 dominated by the stands behind the goals with the stands running along the sides of the ground being two-tiered. The Sky Blue Army of over 3,300, which had quickly sold out, were in the lower tier of the Steve Bull stand which runs the length of the pitch. This made for the most ineffective atmosphere. Many Coventry supporters have questioned why wasn't the away fans at the Ricoh positioned out of the way in a similar manner?

Results
19 Oct 2013   1-1   League One   (Phillips)

Some of the Wolves fans' websites described the SBA celebrations, after Aaron Phillips' equalised, were as if we had won the Champions League.

Pub

Many of the town centre pubs were designated home fans only for our much awaited league visit in October 2013. Our designated pub the **Newhampton Inn,** was 1.6 miles from the station and a mile past the ground. Those in taxis passed Molineux on the way to the pub.

When I contacted the landlord Bill before the game, he said he didn't usually get away supporters but was looking forward to the CCLSC visit. He described the Wolves fans who frequented the Newhampton as *"more Billy Wright than South Bank"*. I think he was referring to the type of people who sit in those stands and not their age.

The landlord opened up the Smoke Room for us Cov fans; he even lit a real fire. Unfortunately, it wasn't as cold as predicted and we all cooked. The estate pub was a delight, a true local pub, and a surprise with its crown green bowling and large garden. Many members were very impressed with the range of beers and excellent (and cheap) home cooked food. The landlady had prepared her own meat pies, as a result of the numbers of CCLSC members I mentioned would be attending,

The Newhampton had eight hand pumps offering seven real ales and a traditional cider. Beers included Caledonian Deuchars IPA, Courage Best Bitter, Enville Ale, Fuller's London Pride, Timothy Taylor Landlord and Wye Valley HPA.

Wycombe Wanderers
Ground – Adams Park

While Adams Park is by no means the only out of town football ground there are few that have more of a middle of nowhere feel to it. While the ground is only 2.5 miles from the town centre it's down a dead end road, past an industrial estate with views of rolling fields beyond. As modern builds go it's not a bad ground with the impressive two tiered Frank Adams Stand running the length of the pitch dominating the stadium. The old main stand runs along the opposite side of the pitch and behind the goal at the Valley End is a standing area for home fans. As part of the planning restriction imposed on the ground the total capacity cannot exceed 10,000. Wycombe, as Coventry City supporters know, used to ground share with Wasps so the pitch took a bit of a battering over the course of a season. The Sky Blue Army were in the Stand behind the goal (pictured).

Results

02 Sep 2014	1-0	Johnstones	(McQuoid)
09 Nov 2016	4-2	FL Trophy	(Haynes 2, Thomas, Bigirimana)
27 Feb 2018	1-0	League Two	(McNulty)
01 Jan 2019	2-0	League One	(Chaplin, Clarke-Harris)
29 Dec 2019	4-1	League One	(Godden 3, McCallum)

Pub

Our visits to Wycombe have been very successful on the pitch, with five wins out of five, but we have had probably our worst pub experiences when visiting High Wycombe. It may not have helped that we never played them on a Saturday afternoon.

For the Johnstone Paint Trophy game in September 2014, with the evening kick off and the fact that the ground is in the middle of nowhere, we met at the **Hour Glass**. It is about a mile from the ground and is the only pub within the Sands area of High Wycombe.

Following a request at the AGM to find pubs near to the ground for evening kick offs, I must admit the Hour Glass wasn't up to our normal pub standards, with its limited availability of real ale. Although Barry Chattaway and Mark White, who was over from the Cayman Islands, were certainly made welcome after the game as they sat and chatted to the landlord.

Nine academy players were on the pitch that night and the SBA were a little unkind with its chants of "1-0 to the under 9's". Although as the saying goes, you know you are

getting older when the police and players look that young! A young looking Ross, Jay and Simon pictured that night.

Despite our poor experience at the Hour Glass we did return for the FL Trophy game in November 2016. The limited range of beers was evident again. Losing at half time we made all three substitutions from the restart, bringing on Jodi Jones, Gael Bigirimana and Ryan Haynes. The latter made an horrendous error to gift Wycombe a second but then got into a number of advanced positions to score a brace himself and an assist in a very entertaining 4-2 win.

Our visit in February 2018 was another evening fixture, and some members from around the South East understandably declined to travel to Wycombe due to the awful weather conditions. Those that did brave the extremely cold weather went back to the Hour Glass. Our policy of meeting at a pub near the ground before evening games didn't prove a success. There was only one real ale being served and several members had to take back their initial pints. The staff did change the beers without complaint before the barrel was changed. We all hoped after our third visit that when we next played at Wycombe, it would be a Saturday and we could meet at a town centre pub with a range of real ale.

For New Year's Day 2019, it was to be a strange start to the year. The visit to Wycombe was the first visit for a 3pm kick-off in modern times. Upon arrival the designated pub, the Bootlegger, wasn't open. This was a pity as it was opposite the station and served up to 10 changing ales and reportedly up to 300+ worldwide beers, with a comprehensive descriptive menu with taste notes available.

I had been unable to contact the pub by phone, email, Facebook, or Twitter over the Xmas period and there had been a recent comment on Trip Advisor that the pub wasn't keeping to its advertised opening times. We had asked members intending on joining us to let me know so I could add them to the WhatsApp group, so if we needed to move to another pub they could be notified. John Burgess who was travelling independently, found the Bootlegger open, but empty at 1pm. New Years Eve has been extremely busy they said and they just hadn't bothered to open up on time the following day.

So it was a pleasant pre match lunchtime drink with other groups of Sky Blues supporters at the local Wetherspoon pub, **The Falcon,** in Cornmarket, in the town centre. We were able to order taxis easily despite it being New Years's Day to get us out to the ground.

It was a Sunday 3pm kick off over the Christmas period on 29 December 2019. The Bootlegger had closed by then, and both member Russ Murden, who lives locally and the local Branch of CAMRA recommended the **Belle Vue**.

It is reached by leaving the station by walking down the London facing platform rather than exiting out the main entrance. It has been in the CAMRA Good Beer Guide for the last 10 years. It is locally valued and is listed as an asset of community value.

Alan, the landlord, said we were welcome to order food in or bring food into the pub, as they do not do food themselves on a Sunday. The Belle Vue opened that Sunday at noon and some members arriving earlier and wanting food, went to the Falcon, which was open and serving their normal food range.

The Belle Vue was normally meant to serve up to six real ales and 4 ciders. It must be Wycombe, but that Sunday within minutes of opening, first one, then two and then a third beer ran out. Only a stout beer remained. Beers were not ready and hadn't been raked after the Saturday evening event with a live band. It was a big disappointment.

Knowing the ground is down a long road through an industrial estate, Phil Higgins, who had driven, left with Eric, Barry and Kevin for the ground early. Eric isn't able to walk very far these days and they wanted to get as close to the ground as possible.

Taxis for everyone else worked but the traffic meant they disembarked around the Hour Glass and everyone walked the 20 minutes to the ground. Phil in his car got stuck in the almost stationary traffic attempting to get closer to the ground. A few members used the football special bus to get back to the station after the game whilst others walked back past the Hour Glass to find their taxis.

As to the football we tamed the "Beast" that day. But wow, what a performance at Wycombe. There was only one team playing football. Wycombe's only tactic was the long ball to Akinfenwa. Kyle McFadzean had him in his pocket, Matty Godden scored a hat trick, Sam McCallum started the scoring with a right foot shot from outside the box. The SBA were fantastic, selling out the away end yet again and were loud from start to finish. Mary, Julie and Jane pictured.

Yeovil Town
Ground – Huish Park

Huish Park has terracing at both ends and two covered, seated sides. The ground, with a capacity of 9,500 is unremarkable and small-scale, but the club's green and white colours are everywhere and this gives it a different look. Most of the Sky Blues Army were standing in the open terrace, (pictured) behind one of the goals.

Results
18 Aug 2012	1-1	League One	(McDonald)
24 Jan 2015	0-0	League One	
06 Oct 2015	0-0	Johnstones Paint	
26 Aug 2017	0-2	League Two	

Our first away game in League One took us to Huist Park, Yeovil. It was the first time the clubs had met in League football. For those travelling by train, Yeovil Junction is 2 miles out of town and 4 to 5 miles from the ground. This is probably the furthest ground-to-station distance of the 92 League teams. Members travelling with the organised CCLSC trip were met at Yeovil Junction by two pre arranged 12 seater minibuses. There were a number of other City fans who, having joined that train at various stations from London, were caught out upon arrival at Yeovil Junction. It is just that, a railway junction several miles from anywhere and it doesn't have a taxi rank.

Pub

The minibuses took us to the **Quicksilver Mail** for lunch and pre match drinks. It served Butcombe, Dartmoor and Sharp's beers. The Quicksilver is a roadside pub with a unique name, which commemorates a high speed mail coach. The large single bar is separate from a lower

dining area. The Mail is about half way between Yeovil Junction and the ground. Pete the landlord a keen football fan, provided a football menu, which we ordered from the train and he reserved the majority of the lower dining area for us.

Over 2,100 fans made the journey to Yeovil that hot August day, with many City fans having a difficult journey to Somerset due to road traffic congestion. Barry arrived late but had time for a pint and to distribute the match tickets.

Rod Dean and Jon Strange didn't arrive at the ground until just before kickoff and couldn't get a pint in before the match.

The minibuses picked us up at 2.30pm to take us to the ground. Police control would not allow them to pick us up afterwards outside the ground, so we walked to the only pub in the area, the Arrow, a large estate pub, for a post match drink before being driven back to Yeovil Junction.

The Arrow had been so packed with the SBA that lunchtime that it was taking an age to get served before the game and many couldn't get food. We of course, had an area to ourselves and enjoyed the fine ales at the Mail.

The journey home saw the train back split at Basingstoke, with only the front three carriages going onto Waterloo. Tim Fisher and Steve Waggott found themselves in the wrong section of the train and so walking through the train stopped at our seats for a chat. They both then stood all the way back to Waterloo sharing beers, chit chat and good humoured banter.

We would be welcomed back in January 2015. Unfortunately, with the increasing demise of our club our support was dwindling. There was only a group of 9 of us on the train this time but we were welcomed back. There was a few more travelling by car. Engineering works around Wimbledon ensured a journey time to Yeovil of over three hours each way. Pete, the Landlord, was away but we were looked after by Tracy who had reserved tables for us in the bar. We were informed that two couples, both Coventry supporters, were staying at the Mail over the weekend. The group is pictured on the next page.

A few members attended the Johnstones Paint game in 2015 and had pre match drinks at the Arrow near the ground.

For our last visit in August 2017, as in previous visits to Yeovil, we organised for prearranged taxis and lunch at the excellent Quicksilver Mail, where we were once again well looked after. Our numbers were down that day, with three members pulling out on the morning of the trip due to illness. It did seem strange that there was no Barry or Colin, who were both unable to travel for family reasons.

York City
Ground – Bootham Crescent

The ground, which holds 8,000 had a tall stand on one side of pitch that only went about two thirds of the way along the length of the pitch. The toilets for men seem to have been there since the ground opened. The urinals were open air and of the 'stand up against a brick wall variety', whilst women have a portable toilet block affair. The Sky Blue Army were accommodated on an open terrace and in the covered Popular Stand on the side of the pitch.

Results
09 Oct 2012   4-0   Johnstones Paint (McGoldrick 2, Ball, Hussey)

We played at York City in October 2012 in the Johnstone Paint Trophy. A 4-0 win sounded easier than it was, with the second only being scored in the 72 minute. David McGoldrick got his second in the 81st and substitute Chris Hussey completed the scoring in the last minute.

Pub

There was no official CCLSC trip for this mid week game, but Jim McIlwaine recalls the day. He met up with Bob Kane, Kev Monks and Rachel and they visited the recommended pub, the Wonky Donkey (aka **The Three Legged Mare)**, in the old town which had a great range of York Brewery ales. They arrived early so visited amongst others the Belgium Beer-House of Trembling Madness which as you can imagine sold some strong lethal beers. They also went to the York Brewery and pubs like the Hole in the Wall and the Lamb & Lion. There were so many excellent pubs in York to visit.

Kev and Rachel pictured.

APPENDIX A

To try and give the reader some perspective and provide some football background I have included some historical data compiled by Jim Brown, a CCLSC Honorary member and the Club's official historian. For a CCLSC context I have included the Player of the Season Awards based on votes cast by members for each match throughout the season. The group photo is at the presentation for Liam Kelly in 2019.

Jim Brown pictured below with me at a Diamond Club luncheon at the Ricoh.

Season 2012-2013

playing at Ricoh Arena, Coventry

League One	**15th**
FA Cup	**3rd Round v Tottenham**
League Cup	**3rd Round v Arsenal**
Trophy	**Area Final v Crewe Alexandra**
Manager	**Andy Thorn (until 26 March)**
	Mark Robins (19 September to 14 February)
	Steve Pressley (from 8 March)

Off the field shenanigans took the spotlight for most of the 2012-13 season and blurred what by Coventry City standards was a good season. The final position of 15th in League One was the lowest finishing position since 1960-61 when the Bantams finished 15th in the old Division Three. The Sky Blues gathered 65 points (reduced to 55 by the 10 points deduction for going into administration) during the season. This equalled the second highest total by a City team since three points for a win was introduced – the highest being 66 in 2001-02.

David McGoldrick was the top scorer with 16. He was to score in seven consecutive away league games (all victories). Leon Clarke became the first player to score for and against the Sky Blues in the same season since Dion Dublin in 1998-99. Clarke had played for Scunthorpe before joining the Sky Blues in January.

The home record was won 7, drew 7, and lost 9. The total of 28 points was the lowest at home since 2002-03 (24 points) but some way off the all-time low of 19 set in the 2001 relegation.

The away form was nothing short of staggering winning 11, drawing 4 and losing 8. For the travelling supporter it was the best season ever with the record-breaking 11 league victories, a club record, topping the 10 wins in 1969-70. 37 points was also a new club record. There were some amazing highs at Milton Keynes, Hartlepool and Doncaster not forgetting historic trips to Arsenal and Spurs. The away goal difference (37-32) was the first positive difference since 2003-04 and only the sixth time in 87 seasons of league football.

City's tremendous away following, no doubt boosted by new grounds and the away form, actually increased from around 900 per game to almost 1200 (the second highest in the division) with almost 5,000 travelling to Milton Keynes. In Cup games 8,000 City fans travelled to Arsenal and 5,000 to Spurs that season.

City played at seven grounds for the first time in competitive games. It was the first ever visits to Yeovil, Stevenage, MK Dons, Crawley and Dagenham & Redbridge. In addition they visited the new grounds of Shrewsbury and Colchester.

Player of the Season

Pictured here, Ian Davidson (right) and Christian Cation (left) presented **Carl Baker** with the CCLSC Player of the Year award after the Orient game. Carl Baker received votes in 69% of the games played this season and achieved the highest number of votes awarded in any single match, when he received 76 votes at the Preston JPT game.

Season 2013 -2014

playing at Sixfields Stadium, Northampton

League One	**18th**
FA Cup	**4th Round v Arsenal**
League Cup	**1st Round v Leyton Orient**
Trophy	**2nd Round v Leyton Orient**

Manager   **Steve Pressley**

The season was played at Sixfields, the home of Northampton Town. It was an exciting season on the field. Callum Wilson was to score 21 league goals, which was especially remarkable considering he missed nine weeks of the season after injuring his shoulder on New Year's Day. It was an exciting campaign when compared with the many sterile seasons, not to mention a couple of relegation battles, since the club left the Premiership in 2001.

The Sky Blues gathered 61 points (reduced to 51 by the 10 points deduction) during the season. This was four less than in 2012-13. The final position of 18th was the lowest finishing position since 1958-59 when the Bantams spent their one and only season in the old Division Four. But for the points deduction a final position of 9th would have been achieved.

The home record was won 9, drew 8, and losing 6. The total of 35 points was the best at home since 2006-07 (37 points). The goals scored (41) was the highest since 1978-79 but the goals conceded (39) was the highest in the club's Football League history. The away form (7 wins, 26 points) whilst not up to the previous season's record-breaking 11 wins and 37 points, was still the fourth best since the club were relegated from the Premier League.

It will be no surprise to discover that the home average attendance of 2,364 (boosted by sell out away followings from Wolves, Sheffield United and Peterborough) was the lowest in the club's Football League history and you have to go back to the Birmingham League days of 1905-06 to find a lower average. Only three clubs in the League had a lower average in the league. City's tremendous away following increased by

40% to 1603 – the second highest in the division and beaten by only six Championship clubs.

City played at only two grounds for the first time in competitive games. The Cup game was the first visit to AFC Wimbledon's ground in Kingston and, before this season, they had not appeared at Sixfields.

Player of the Season

Joe Murphy was the winner of the 2013-14 Player of the Season. There was no formal presentation at the end of the season, due to the team playing at Northampton. We hoped to present the award to Joe at one of the pre-season friendlies before the start of next season. However, Joe had left the Club for Huddersfield by then and Steve Pressley accepted the trophy from Kev Monks on his behalf at the pre-season friendly at Stevenage. Members Phil Smith and Barry Chattaway made a detour on the way to the Barnsley midweek game to drop off the trophy at the Huddersfield training ground.

Murphy joined the CCLSC Hall of Fame which has many of the Sky Blue greats who have won this prestigious award in the past, including goalkeepers Steve Ogrizovic 'Oggy', who won the award in 1995 and 1997, and Westwood in 2010. Joe certainly showed the value of goalkeepers by receiving votes from in 74% of the games played this season.

Season 2014 -2015

playing at Sixfields Stadium, Northampton before returning to Ricoh Arena, Coventry on 21 August

League One	**17th**
FA Cup	**1st Round v Worcester City**
League Cup	**1st Round v Cardiff City**
Trophy	**Area Semi Final v Bristol City**
Manager	**Steve Pressley (until 23 February)**
	Tony Mowbray (from 3 March)

Even by Coventry City's standards the 2014-15 season was depressing. Home fans saw only six league victories (five if they didn't go to Sixfields) and relegation fears from League One hung over the club from February right through to the last ten minutes in the final game at Crawley.

Ultimately it was the club's away form (7 wins, 28 points) which kept the club up. They were unbeaten in the last six away games, with four wins and four clean sheets in a row (the best run of away shut-outs in the club's history).

City found goalscoring difficult. Frank Nouble topped the lists with seven goals (6 league, 1 JPT). Two other players (Jim O'Brien and Dominic Samuel) also scored six league goals.

For league games City's away following averaged 1,002 – a decrease of 37% – but still the sixth highest in the division.

City played at two grounds for the first time, both within four days in March, and won both. They had never visited Chesterfield's new ground, the Proact Stadium, before. The last time City played in the town was in 1960 when Chesterfield played at Saltergate. Four days later City visited Fleetwood's Highbury Stadium for the first time.

Player of the Season

Members Adrian Hawthorne and Phil Smith presented the 2014/15 Award to **Jim O'Brien** after the Crewe game (pictured). Jim became the first Scottish player to win the trophy since Gary McAllister in 2000. Previous winners include other north of the border greats Tommy Hutchison, Gary Gillespie, David Speedie and Kevin Gallacher. He received votes from CCLSC members in 40 out of 49 of the games played this season, achieved 7 consecutive Man of the Match awards which included every league game in October, and achieved the highest number of votes awarded in any single match, when he received 95 votes at the Orient away game in November.

Season 2015-2016

playing at Ricoh Arena, Coventry

League One	**8th**
FA Cup	**1st Round v Northampton Town**
League Cup	**1st Round v Rochdale**
Trophy	**2nd Round v Yeovil Town**
Manager	**Tony Mowbray**

After having to come from behind to win at Crawley to retain League One status at the end of the previous season, the first-half of this season was remarkable and City were top of the pile after 20 games. The Sky Blues went unbeaten in eleven league games after losing at Bury in September before losing at Bramall Lane on 13 December. Expectations rocketed but a miserable March with four consecutive defeats cost City dearly. The final position of 8th was the first top half finish since 2005-06.

The Sky Blues gathered 69 league points during the season. The home record was much improved: winning 12, drawing 6, and losing 5. The five defeats suffered at home was the lowest for a home season since 2005-06 (four). The away record: won 7, drew 6, lost 10, and earned 27 points, one short on the previous season.

The biggest win of the season was the 6-0 home victory over Bury in February which was the biggest league win since the 8-1 thrashing of Shrewsbury in 1963 and the first 'six' at home since Derby were defeated 6-1 in 2005-06. The 5-0 win at Crewe was the biggest away win for three years – since they won by the same score at Hartlepool.

On three occasions the Sky Blues scored four goals without reply in the first-half: Gillingham (h), Crewe (a) and Bury (h). This had only happened twice in the last 50 years (v Derby in the last game at Highfield Road in 2005 and v Preston a year earlier).

Adam Armstrong was leading scorer with 20 goals, all in the league. Armstrong was only the third player in the last 49 years to score 20 or more league goals, following in the footsteps of Ian Wallace (21 in 1977-78) and Callum Wilson (21 in 2013-14)

For league games City's away following averaged 1,339.

City played at Burton Albion's Pirelli Stadium for the first time and came away with three points, one of only two teams to win there this season.

Player of the Season

Member Rob Parker presented the 2015/16 Award to **Romain Vincelot** after the game against Sheffield United (pictured). Romain received votes from CCLSC members in 38 out of 46 of the games played this season. He was to become the first Frenchman to win the award.

Season 2016-2017

playing at Ricoh Arena, Coventry

League One	**23rd (relegated)**
FA Cup	**2nd Round v Cambridge United**
League Cup	**2nd Round v Norwich City**
Trophy	**Winners v Oxford United**
Manager	**Tony Mowbray (until 29 September)**
	Russell Slade (from 21 Dec to 5 Mar)
	Mark Robins (from 6 March)

The final position of 23rd was fifteen places lower than 2015/16 and confirmed the club's third relegation of the 21st century (after 49 years without one). Statistically it was not just the worst season in living memory but the worst since the club was elected to the Football League in 1919. There were few highlights with the majority coming in the much-maligned Checkatrade Trophy which the Sky Blues, rejuvenated by the arrival of Mark Robins, won in style on a magical day at Wembley.

The Sky Blues gathered 39 league points during the season. By City's standards, the home record wasn't that bad: won 8, drew 7, losing 8. The eight defeats came in a run of 10 games between November and March sandwiched between two unbeaten runs of eight and five games respectively. The away record: won 1, drew 5, lost 17, and earned only 8 points, the lowest total since 1999/2000. The 17 defeats were the worst since 1925/26 when 18 losses were incurred.

George Thomas was leading scorer with nine goals, five in the league and four in the Checkatrade Trophy.

For league games City's away following averaged 814 (2015/16 1,339), a drop of 39% and the lowest since 2010/11. Of course, City's following at Wembley surpassed everything with 43,268 the official number of Sky Blues supporters who attended.

City played competitive games at three grounds for the first time - Oxford United's Kassam Stadium, Bristol Rovers'

Memorial Stadium and the New Wembley. In addition they played a league game at AFC Wimbledon for the first time and at Northampton's Sixfields Stadium for the first time as an away team.

Player of the Season

Member Alastair Laurie presented the 2016/17 Award to **Gael Bigirimana** after the Walsall game (pictured). He was the CCLSC man of the match on 13 occasions (more than double that of any other player) and voted in the top three in over 20 games. Gael joins Peter Ndlovu, who won the award in 1992/93, to become the second African born player to win the award.

Season 2017-2018

playing at Ricoh, Coventry

League Two	**6th (promoted via the Play Offs)**
FA Cup	**5th Round v Brighton**
League Cup	**1st Round v Blackburn Rovers**
Trophy	**Group stage**
Manager	**Mark Robins**

There was an upturn in the club's fortunes. Promotion from League Two, despite finishing sixth, the best FA Cup run for nine years, with the Premiership scalp of Stoke City in round three, not to mention a new goalscoring hero in the shape of 28-goal Marc McNulty who outscored many of the striker heroes of the past fifty years. McNulty scored more league goals than any player since Bobby Gould hit 24 in the 1966-67 promotion campaign. His total goals are the best since George Hudson netted the same number in all competitions in 1963-64. Terry Bly scored 29 in 1962-63.

The Sky Blues gathered 75 league points during the season – the first time the club has reached 70 points in a season since that three points for a win was introduced in 1981. The final position of 6th was the highest final position since 6th place in the old Division One in 1969-70.

The home record was 13 wins, 4 draws and 6 losses. 13 home wins was the best haul since 1986-87 when 14 were won (out of 21 games). 43 points equals the number won in 2005-06 which was the best since 1986-87. The defeats were largely surprising – to the two promoted clubs, Newport and Forest Green, and the 6-2 debacle against Yeovil. The club recorded eight consecutive home wins between December and February, the club's best run since 1954.

Away from home the record read 9 wins, 5 draws, 9 losses. After winning only 8 away points the previous season this was a massive improvement and the third highest total of away wins in the club's history.

For league games City's away following averaged 1,268 (2016/17 806), an increase of 57%.

City played competitive games at five grounds for the first time: Barnet's Hive Stadium, Accrington's Crown Ground, Forest Green's New Lawn, Rodney Parade, Newport and Whaddon Road, Cheltenham. In addition they played a league game at Cambridge United for the first time.

Player of the Season

Member Kevin Randall presented the 2017/18 Award to **Michael Doyle** after the Morecambe game (pictured). Michael Doyle received a record number of 899 votes. He was voted in the top three in an incredible 46 out of 47 games. Not surprising when you recall his goal from the half way line, his quick free kicks and the encouragement he provided the rest of the team! The complete Captain Fantastic!

Season 2018-2019

playing at Ricoh Arena, Coventry

League One	**8th**
FA Cup	**1st Round v Walsall**
League Cup	**1st Round v Oxford United**
Trophy	**Group stages**
Manager	**Mark Robins**

After promotion from League Two in 2017-18 this was a season of consolidation for the Sky Blues and everyone can feel satisfied with an eighth place finish in League One. The Sky Blues gathered 65 league points during the season – ten points less than 2017-18 but still the third best haul in the last 17 years.

At home there were 9 wins, 7 draws and 7 losses. After last season's 13 home wins this was a disappointing home campaign with only 34 points gained. Another great season on the road and the third highest total of away wins in the club's history saw 9 wins, 5 draws and 10 losses.

Jordy Hiwula was leading scorer with 13 goals, 12 in the league, and one in the EFL Trophy. After McNulty's goal glut last season it sounds a poor return but he would have led the scoring charts in all of the six seasons between 2006-2012.

For league games City's away following averaged 1,315 (2016/17 1,268), an increase of 3%. The best league following of the season was 2,683 at Sunderland, one of the longest away trips of the season.

The 5-4 win at Sunderland has to be the game of the season. It was the sixth time City have been on the winning side in a 5-4 game and the first away from home. The Sky Blues ended Sunderland's 23 game unbeaten run and inflicted the Black Cats first home defeat of the season.

Player of the Season

Member Phil Higgins presented the CCLSC Player of the Season Award to **Liam Kelly** after the Shrewsbury match. Pictured. It was one of the closest competitions for several years. There were 33 different players who received votes throughout the season. Going into April, Liam was some 170 votes behind Jordon Willis and Luke Thomas, who had shared the top spot between them since December.

Kelly had a remarkable second half of the season. He was voted in the top three for 20 of the last 24 matches. He didn't appear in the top 6 until March and had only received votes in three matches up until November.

Liam joined an illustrious group of past winners of the CCLSC Player of the Season. He joins the likes of Tommy Hutchison, Cyrille Regis, David Speedie, Steve Ogrizovic, Gary McSheffrey, among others and more recently midfield favourites, Carl Baker, Jim O'Brien, Gael Bigirimana and last season's winner, Michael Doyle.

Season 2019-2020

playing at St Andrews, Birmingham

League One	**Champions**
FA Cup	**4th Round v Birmingham City**
League Cup	**2nd Round v Watford**
Trophy	**2nd Round v MK Dons**
Manager	**Mark Robins**

Coventry City were to be Champions of a division for only the fourth time in 94 seasons in the Football League (1936, 1964, 1967 and 2020). From 34 League One games the Sky Blues gathered 67 points – two points more than 2018-19 but still the third best haul since three points for a win was introduced in 1981. A new term 'points per game' (PPG) entered the football vocabulary because of the curtailed season. City's PPG was 1.971 and was the highest in the club's League history, topping 1966-67 when after adjusting for three points the PPG was 1.952.

An outstanding home record was the cornerstone to the Sky Blues' season 11 wins, 5 draws, 1 loss. If the season had been completed the number of victories would have beaten the best since 1967 which was 14 in 1986-87. Whilst the home form set the foundations of a successful season it was the away form, especially after Christmas with a staggering seven away wins out of eight that took the Sky Blues out of and away from the pack. The lowest number of away losses in a season before this was five (1967 and 1989) and few City fans can think that this record would have not been broken if the season had been completed.

Matt Godden was leading scorer with 15 goals, 14 in the league, and one in the League Cup.

For league games City's away following averaged 1,876 (2018/19 1,315), an increase of 42%.

There were many fantastic games in this memorable season, the home comeback to beat Blackpool, the nine-man comeback at Portsmouth, the Cup win at Ipswich but Jim

Brown's vote went to the 4-1 victory at Wycombe. Wycombe were league leaders and unbeaten at home and the Sky Blues demolished them. It was the day that many City fans realised that promotion was a strong possibility.

Player of the Season

CCLSC announced **Fankaty Dabo** as our Player of the Season for 2019/20 in our June newsletter. With the Covid pandemic restricting player and supporter gatherings we were not able to formally present Fanky with his award at the usual end of season ceremony.

With agreement from the Club, Fanky's Father Mohammed, a CCLSC member, made the presentation at a family gathering (pictured). At the time of writing we are still looking forward to organising a social event attended by members, to congratulate Fanky on his award.

Fankaty Dabo incredibly received votes in 37 different matches during the season. Fanky is not in bad company. Other full backs and past winners of the CCLSC Player of the Season Award include Danny Thomas (1982), Stuart Pearce (1985) and Richard Keogh (2011 and 2012).

APPENDIX B

CCLSC Player of the Season Awards

Season	Winner	Presenter(s)
2012/13	Carl Baker	Ian Davidson/ Christian Cation
2013/14	Joe Murphy	Kev Monks
2014/15	Jim O'Brien	Adrian Hawthorne/ Phil Smith
2015/16	Romain Vincelo	Rob Parker
2016/17	Gael Bigirimana	Alastair Laurie
2017/18	Michael Doyle	Kevin Randall
2018/19	Liam Kelly	Phil Higgins
2019/20	Fankaty Dabo	Mohammed Dabo

APPENDIX C

CCLSC Forecasting Competition

Season	Winners	Runner Up
2012/13 (37)	Mark Davidson (103)	Steve Woodfield (95)
2013/14 (37)	Steve Woodfiled (103)	Rod Dean (99)
2014/15 (61)	Robin Morden (100)	Christian Mullen (94)
2015/16 (59)	Julian Foster (105)	Sara Robb (104)
2016/17 (70)	Scott Harbertson (121)	Simon Fahy (113)
2017/18 (87)	Christine Davidson (120)	Rob Stevens (107)
2018/19 (94)	Bob Mankin (107)	Jason Hall (99)
2019/20 (90)	Eric Whiting (93)	Alan Plumb (88)

For the 2020/21 season we had a record 105 entries.

Notes

    a) The number of entries each season shown in brackets after the season

    b) The individuals points scored are shown in brackets after their name

Competition Rules

Points are allocated as follows:

6 points = correct result with BOTH teams scores correct
4 points = correct result with ONE teams score correct
3 points = correct result with NO score correct
1 points = incorrect result with ONE score correct
0 points = incorrect result and NO scores correct

APPENDIX D

40th Anniversary Dinner

On Thursday 17 November CCLSC celebrated their 40th Anniversary at the Wharfside Bar near London Bridge. It was attended by 55 members and guests who enjoyed an excellent three course meal. The evening was impeccably MC'd throughout by our social secretary Kevin Mofid (photo opposite)

Former player Chris Cattlin was the guest speaker and he was entertaining with some very funny and interesting stories from his time at Coventry City and his time as a footballer, manager and businessman.

During the evening Kevin also read out a personal message from John Sillett who apologised for not being able to attend as he was recovering from an operation. In his message, John recalled his happy memories of meeting CCLSC members over the years.

The raffle on the evening made over £1,000 for the Alzhiemer's Association.

APPENDIX E

CCLSC Q & A Evening Socials

Over these years we have held several Q&As with Club officials. These are held at the Calthorpe Arms, near Kings Cross in central London.

We were host to Tim Fisher at a meeting in London in May 2013. The Coventry City chief executive spoke and replied to questions about the current situation surrounding the football club. The ninety-minute meeting, arranged at short notice, attracted thirty-two members. Very detailed minutes of the meeting were issued to members and these included the statement that Tim suggested "They should put a statue of Joy Seppala outside the ground for the £45m she has put into the club". This statement was to be recited overtime by many other supporter groups.

Interestingly, much of what Tim Fisher outlined to members that evening was proved to be true as the sorry history unfolded over the coming years.

Tim Fisher was to return on a number of times to speak with members. Steve Waggott and Chris Anderson, in their time as Chairman or CEO of the Club also attended evening social Q&As. The intention of these meetings was not to go over the historical events but to concentrate on the current situation and the future of our football club.

In December 2015, the then Manager, Tony Mowbray attended. It was literally standing room only at the Calthorpe Arms for the Q&A. Members comments ranged from "a great evening" to "one of the best events for years".

Tony Mowbray spoke for over 2 hours in front of the 50 members in attendance. He was uplifting, insightful and inspiring.

 It seemed at times as if he was conducting a training session as he spoke passionately about all things football from loans, the U21 league, players, tactics, injuries and contracts. And before anyone asks, no, he wouldn't give away any confidential information. He also discussed that big "what if we got promoted" and said he would like to be invited back to speak to us again for our promotion party. We certainly would have liked that but our season deteriorated after Christmas and the hopes of promotion disappeared.

In January 2018, at a packed to capacity Calthorpe Arms, Mark Robins and Dave Boddy became the latest in a long line of Managers and Club officials to attend a CCLSC social evening

Dave addressed the question of the Club's current situation and Mark discussed his approach to recruitment and developing of players, his approach to tactics, and when and how to bring on the academy players. He was very complementary about the SBA support specifically mentioning the Play-Off Second Leg game at Notts County and the Final at Wembley.

Pictured below with Mark Robins are Barry and Rob, receiving his raffle prize.

Mark ended the evening by giving his account of the day "he is reported to have saved Fergie's job". Whilst never actually confirming or denying whether he did or not, he instead referred to how his memory of the goal differed from that in the Sir Alex's autobiography.

Members were treated to a very enjoyable evening in November 2019 in the company of Sky Blues legend and CCLSC Patron Steve Ogrizovic (known to many as Oggy). He highlighted key games, the Tottenham away game, to keep us in the Premier League, his last but one game against Arsenal, and of course the Cup Final. There were several questions about that day in May 1987.

Steve recalled a few things about the day. John Sillett saying to keep it tight for the first 15 minutes (that went well didn't it, he joked), the mix up with Trevor Peake, which fortunately Glenn Hoodle didn't take advantage of, and not wanting to let down the mass of Sky Blue in the stadium. He recalled the celebrations afterwards, that night and back in Coventry over the next few days.

Most people recall Clive Allen scoring in the first couple of minutes, his 49th of the season. Steve was very clear it was 1 minute 58 seconds. Somehow it stuck in his memory.

APPENDIX F

Diamond Club

The Coventry City Diamond Club is for supporters with fifty or more service following the Sky Blues. Quarterly luncheons have been held at the Ricoh and are attended by as many as 200 members. CCLSC has taken a table at the Diamond Club quarterly luncheon for the last few years.

There are a number of CCLSC members who are also Diamond Club committee members. In fact, Kev Randall, CCLSC's Treasurer is Vice Chair of the Diamond Club. Members Barry Chattaway, Kev Monks and Honorary Member Jenny Poole serve as Diamond Club Committee Members.

With the Diamond Club luncheons usually taking place on a Thursday one of the silver linings was that travellers could use the Coventry to the Ricoh Arena train service. This as we know hasn't been that reliable on match days. The London train would arrive into Coventry station with a few minutes to spare enabling a group of us to use the shuttle service. Phil Smith travelling from Bristol and Rod Williams from Milton Keynes would ensure their trains arrived into Coventry to meet the connection. Coventry based Mick Barlow and Eric Whiting would be waiting on the platform at Coventry station to meet us.

After the luncheon there was often time before catching trains home to have a catch up drink at the Gatehouse.

Pictures on the next pages are of a group at the luncheon and with Former Managers, John Sillett and Ron Atkinson. Also at the May 2017 luncheon and to celebrate 30 years from the Wembley win, a group of members were photographed with the FA Cup.

APPENDIX G

Attending U21/23 matches

London and South East based members do not get much opportunity to see the academy players. We have members attend U21/23 matches when they play in the London area. The games are usually played during the week day. This limits numbers able to attend.

With me at Crystal Palace (top photo) are left to right Colin Heys, Martin and Charles.

In the bottom photo are Charles, JB, Rod, and Martin at QPR back in 2014 when we saw a young James Maddison terrorise a Premier League academy team.

APPENDIX H

CCLSC Designated Pubs

Accrington Stanley		36 - 38
Peel Park Hotel	Oct 2017	
Peel Park Hotel	Mar 2019	
AFC Wimbledon		40 - 41
Woodies	Nov 2013	
Antelope	Feb 2017	
Albion	Aug 2018	
Arsenal		42 - 44
Compton Arms	Sep 2012	
Compton Arms	Jan 2014	
Barnet		45 - 46
Metropolitan Bar	Oct 2017	
Barnsley		47 - 49
Old Nn 7	Jan 2014	
Old Nn 7	Mar 2015	
Old Nn 7	Mar 2016	
Silkstone Inn	Mar 2019	
Birmingham City		50
Woodman	Feb 2020	
Blackpool		51 - 53
Bloomfield Brewhouse	Mar 2016	
Bloomfield Brewhouse	Aug 2018	
Pump & Trumpet	Aug 2018	
Bolton Wanderers		54 - 55
Bee Hive	Nov 2016	
Spinning Mule	Aug 2019	
Bournemouth		56 - 57
Cricketers Arms	Feb 2013	
Bradford City		58 - 61
Corn Dolly	Nov 2013	
Corn Dolly	Aug 2014	
Corn Dolly	Aug 2015	
Corn Dolly	Aug 2016	
Corn Dolly	Nov 2018	
Brentford		62 - 63
Magpie & Crown	Oct 2012	
Magpie & Crown	Mar 2014	
Brighton & Hove Albion		64 - 65
Beer Dispensary	Feb 2018	
Bristol City		66 - 67
Merchant Arms	Feb 2014	
Merchant Arms	Dec 2014	
Merchant Arms	Aug 2015	

CCLSC Designated Pubs

Bristol Rovers		68 - 71
Mouse	Dec 2016	
Post Office Tavern	Sep 2018	
Post Office Tavern	Jan 2020	
Post Office Tavern	Feb 2020	
Burton Albion		72 - 76
Old Cottage Tavern	Sep 2015	
Burton Bridge Inn	Nov 2018	
Devonshire Arms	Sep 2019	
Bury		77 - 79
Trackside	Feb 2013	
Trackside	Sep 2015	
Trackside	Feb 2017	
Cambridge United		80 - 82
Devonshire Arms	Dec 2016	
Devonshire Arms	Sep 2017	
Carlisle United		83 - 85
Kings Head	Jan 2013	
Kings Head	Aug 2013	
Howard's Arms	Dec 2017	
Charlton Athletic		86 - 88
White Swan	Oct 2016	
White Swan	Oct 2018	
Cheltenham Town		89 - 91
Kemble Brewery	Apr 2018	
Kemble Brewery	Nov 2018	
Chesterfield		92 - 94
Derby Tup	Mar 2015	
Derby Tup	Dec 2015	
Derby Tup	Jan 2017	
Derby Tup	Sep 2017	
Colchester United		95 - 99
Bricklayers Arms	Nov 2012	
Bricklayers Arms	Mar 2014	
Victoria Inn	Nov 2014	
Victoria inn	Nov 2015	
Victoria Inn	Feb 2018	
Victoria Inn	Nov 2019	
Crawley Town		100 - 104
Swan	Apr 2013	
Swan	Aug 2013	
Snooty Fox	May 2015	
Brewery Shades	Apr 2018	

CCLSC Designated Pubs

Crewe Alexandra		105 - 108
Hops	Sep 2012	
Borough Arms	Feb 2013	
Borough Arms	Mar 2014	
Borough Arms	Oct 2014	
Borough Arms	Jan 2016	
Borough Arms	Mar 2018	
Dagenham & Redbridge		109 - 110
Eastbrook	Aug 2012	
Doncaster Rovers		111 - 113
Corner Pin	Dec 2012	
Corner Pin	Dec 2014	
Corner Pin	Apr 2016	
Corner Pin	May 2019	
The (Little) Plough	Jan 2020	
Exeter City		114 - 115
Mill on the Exe	Jan 2018	
Fleetwood Town		116 - 120
Bisham Hotel	Mar 2015	
Strawberry Gardens	Mar 2015	
Strawberry Gardens	Oct 2015	
Strawberry Gardens	Sep 2016	
Pump & Trumpet	Nov 2018	
Strawberry Gardens	Nov 2018	
Layton Rakes	Jan 2020	
Forest Green Rovers		121 - 123
Ale House	Feb 2018	
Ground	Oct 2019	
Gillingham		124 - 126
Will Adams	Mar 2014	
Will Adams	Jan 2015	
Will Admas	Apr 2016	
Will Adams	Sep 2016	
Will Adams	Aug 2018	
Grimsby Town		127 - 129
Willy's	Aug 2017	
Hartlepool United		130 - 131
Rat Race/Ward Jackson	Nov 2012	
Rat Race/Ward Jackson	Dec 2013	
Ipswich Town		133 - 136
Station Hotel	Dec 2019	
Steamboat Tavern	Mar 2020	
Leyton Orient		137 - 140
King William IV	Oct 2012	
Birkbeck Tavern	Aug 2013	
Birkbeck Tavern	Oct 2013	
Birkbeck Tavern	Jan 2014	
Leyton Technical	Nov 2014	

CCLSC Designated Pubs

CCLSC Designated Pubs

Oxford United		177 - 180
Royal Blenheim	Jun 2013	
Royal Blenheim	Nov 2016	
Seven Stars on Green	Aug 2018	
St Aldates	Sep 2018	
St Aldates	Aug 2019	
Peterborough United		181 - 184
Brewery Tap	Apr 2014	
Brewery Tap	Mar 2015	
Brewery Tap	Mar 2016	
Brewery Tap	Dec 2016	
Brewery Tap	Mar 2019	
Brewery Tap	Oct 2019	
Plymouth Argyle		185 - 187
Fortescue Hotel	Jan 2019	
Portsmouth		188 - 191
Artillery Arms	Mar 2013	
Old House at Home	Jul 2015	
Artillery Arms	Apr 2019	
Artillery Arms	Aug 2019	
John Jacques	Aug 2019	
Port Vale		192 - 196
Bulls Head	Sep 2013	
Bulls Head	Dec 2014	
Bulls Head	Feb 2016	
Bulls Head	Oct 2016	
Bulls Head `	Dec 2017	
Preston North End		197 - 200
Old Black Bull	Jan 2013	
Black Horse	Jan 2014	
Black Horse	Feb 2015	
Rochdale		201 - 206
Cemetery Hotel	Sep 2014	
Cemetery Hotel	Aug 2015	
Cemetery Hotel	Oct 2015	
Cemetery Hotel	Apr 2017	
Baum	Feb 2019	
Baum	Feb 2020	
Rotherham United		207 - 210
Bridge Inn	Jan 2014	
Cutlers Arms	Oct 2019	

CCLSC Designated Pubs

Scunthorpe United		211 - 214
Honest Lawyer	Mar 2014	
Berkeley Hotel	Sep 2014	
Berkeley Hotel	Sep 2015	
Blue Bell	Apr 2017	
Berkeley Hotel	Jan 2019	
Sheffield United		215 - 218
Sheaf View	Feb 2013	
Devonshire Cat	May 2014	
Devonshire Cap	Feb 2015	
Sheffield tap	Dec 2015	
Devonshire Cat	Apr 2017	
Shrewsbury Town		219 - 224
Prince of Wales	Sep 2012	
Three Fishes	Aug 2013	
Three Fishes	Mar 2016	
Three Fishes	Mar 2017	
Coach & Horses	Dec 2018	
Coach & Horses	Dec 2019	
Southend United		225 - 227
Olde Trout Tavern	Jan 2016	
Olde Trout Tavern	Dec 2016	
Olde Trout Tavern	Oct 2018	
Olde Trout Tavern	Feb 2020	
Stevenage		228 - 232
Old Mutual Friend	Dec 2012	
Marquis of Lorne	Oct 2013	
Chequers	Aug 2014	
Chequers	Nov 2017	
Chequers	Jul 2018	
Sunderland		233 - 237
Dun Cow	Apr 2019	
Centurion (Newcastle)	Nov 2019	
Sutton United		238 - 240
Cock & Bull	Jul 2017	
Moon on the Hill	Jul 2018	
Swindon Town		241 -246
Glue Pot	Oct 2012	
Great Western (GW)	Dec 2013	
Great Western (GW)	Aug 2014	
Glue Pot	Oct 2015	
Glue Pot	Aug 2016	
Glue Pot	Sep 2017	
Wyvern Taveren	Aug 2019	

CCLSC Designated Pubs

Lightning Source UK Ltd.
Milton Keynes UK
UKHW022151211220
375676UK00005B/109